AMERICAN VOICES FROM

World War I

World War I

Adriane Ruggiero

BENCHMARK BOOKS

MARSHALL CAVENDISH
NEW YORK

To R, who loved the airplanes

Benchmark Books
Marshall Cavendish
99 White Plains Road
Tarrytown, New York 10591-9001
www.marshallcavendish.com

Text copyright © 2003 by Marshall Cavendish Corporation
Map © 2003 by Marshall Cavendish Corporation
Map by Laszlo Kubinyi

Ruggiero, Adriane.
World War I / by Ruggiero, Adriane.
p. cm. — (American voices from—)
Summary: Presents the history of the U.S. involvement in World War I through excerpts from letters, newspaper articles, speeches and songs dating from the period. Includes bibliographical references and index.
ISBN 0-7614-1203-4

1. World War, 1914–1918—Sources—Juvenile literature. 2. World War, 1914–1918—United States—Sources—Juvenile literature. [1. World War, 1914–1918—Sources. 2. United States—History—1913–1921.] I. Title: World War One. II. Title: World War 1. III. Title. IV. Series.
D522.7 .R84 2002   940.3'73—dc21
2001008747

Printed in Italy
1 3 5 6 4 2

Series design and composition by Anne Scatto / PIXEL PRESS
Art Research by Rose Corbett Gordon, Mystic CT

The photographs in this book are used by permission and through the courtesy of:
Front cover: Bettmann/Corbis; pages ii & 6: Corbis; pages viii, xii, 8, 15, 20. 27, 32, 53, 57, 67, 74, 76, 78, 81, 85, 94, 98: The Granger Collection, New York; pages xiv, xv, xx, xxiii, xxvi, 40, 44, 49, 60, 62, 103: Hulton Archive/Getty Images; pages 10, 26, 35: Stock Montage, Inc.; page 23: The State Historical Society of Wisconsin; page 43: National Museum of American History, Armed Forces; page 72: National Archives

ON THE COVER: War rally in New York City, August 31, 1917

ON THE TITLE PAGE: *Flag Day*, 1918, by Childe Hassam

Acknowledgments

Permission has been granted to use quotations from the following copyrighted works: *Over There: The Story of America's First Great Overseas Crusade* by Frank Freidel; used by permission of Madeleine Freidel. *American Women in World War I: They Also Served* by Lettie Gavin; used by permission of University of Colorado Press. *From a Surgeon's Journal* by Harvey Cushing; used by permission of Little, Brown and Company.

Excerpts from "Harlem" in *You Must Remember This: An Oral History of Manhattan from the 1890s to World War II,* copyright © 1989 by Jeff Kisseloff, reprinted by permission of Harcourt, Inc.

Contents

Will you have a part in Victory?

WRITE TO THE
NATIONAL
WAR GARDEN
COMMISSION ~
WASHINGTON, D.C.
for free books on
gardening, canning
& drying.

© 1918 NATIONAL WAR GARDEN COMMISSION

JAMES MONTGOMERY FLAGG

"Every Garden a Munition Plant"

Charles Lathrop Pack, President

Photographs, paintings, and drawings—like this colorful poster by artist James Montgomery Flagg—are fine examples of primary sources. These keys to the past provide us with a richer, more meaningful understanding of our history.

About Primary Sources

What Is a Primary Source?

In the pages that follow, you will be hearing many different "voices" from a special time in America's past. Some of the selections are long while others are short. You'll find many easy to understand at first reading while some may require several readings. All the selections have one thing in common, however. They are primary sources. This is the name historians give to the bits and pieces of information that make up the record of human existence. Primary sources are important to us because they are the very essence, the core material for all historical investigation. You can call them "history" itself.

Primary sources *are* evidence; they give historians the all-important clues they need to understand the past. Perhaps you have read a detective story in which a sleuth must solve a mystery by piecing together bits of evidence he or she uncovers. The detective makes deductions, or educated guesses based on the evidence, and solves the mystery once all the deductions point in a certain direction. Historians work in much the same way. Like detectives, historians analyze the data by careful reading and rereading. After much analysis, historians draw conclusions about an event, a person, or an entire era. Historians may analyze the same evidence and come to different conclusions. This is why there is often sharp disagreement about an event.

Primary sources are also called *documents*—a rather dry word to describe what can be just about anything: an official speech by a government leader, an old map, an act of Congress, a letter worn out from too much handling, an entry hastily scrawled into a diary, a detailed newspaper account of a tragic event, a funny or sad song, a colorful poster, a cartoon, a faded photograph, or someone's eloquent remembrance captured on tape or film.

By examining the following primary sources, you, the reader, will be taking on the role of historian. Here is your chance to immerse yourself in a specific time—World War I. You'll come to know the voices of the men and women who lived during those years when America took part in its first global war. You'll read the songs they sang, the poems they wrote, the newspaper articles they read, and the words they used to express their thoughts about what was happening around them.

Our language has changed in the decades since that war. The people who lived in the early 1900s were more formal in the way they wrote. Their everyday vocabulary contained many words that will be unfamiliar to someone living in this century. Don't be discouraged! Trying to figure out language is exactly the kind of work a historian does. Like a historian, when your work is done, you will have a deeper, more meaningful understanding of the past.

How to Read a Primary Source

Each document in this book deals with World War I and U.S. involvement in that conflict. Some of the documents are from government archives such as the Library of Congress. Others are from the official papers of major figures in American history. A few of the documents are from the great pool of popular culture that sprang into life during the early 1900s. All of the documents, major and minor, help us to understand what it was like to be alive during the Great War.

As you read each document, ask yourself some basic but important questions. Who was the writer? Who was the writer's audience? What was the writer's point of view? What was he or she trying to tell that audience? Is the message clearly expressed, or is it implied, that is, stated indirectly? What words did the writer use to convey his or her message? Are the words emotion-filled or objective in tone? If you are looking at a photograph, examine it carefully, taking in all the details. Where do you think it was taken? What's happening in the foreground? In the background? Is it posed? Or is it an action shot? How can you tell? Who do you think took the picture? What is its purpose? These are questions that help you think critically about a document.

Some tools have been included with the documents to help you in your historical investigations. Unusual words have been defined near some selections. Thought-provoking questions follow the documents. They help focus your reading so you will get the most out of the primary sources. As you read each selection, you'll probably come up with many questions of your own. That's great! The work of a historian always leads to many, many questions. Some can be answered; others cannot and require further investigation.

Although World War I began in 1914, the United States struggled to stay out of the conflict until 1917, when it could no longer avoid becoming involved. American soldiers are shown firing at the enemy in this 1918 photograph.

Introduction

A WORLD AT WAR

The First World War (1914–1918) is called a world war because it was fought on several continents. Although most of the fighting took place in Europe, the conflict was also carried out in the Middle East and in Africa. The First World War was also the first major war of the twentieth century. It was followed after a brief time by yet another world conflict of even larger scale—the Second World War (1939–1945).

For the nations of Europe, World War I was a tragedy. It could have been prevented and the lives of millions spared. But war broke out, and national leaders sent their youth off to fight—and to die. The cost was terrible. During one battle alone, the Battle of the Somme, 420,000 British, 195,000 French, and 600,000 German soldiers were killed over a four-month period.

At the end of four years of fighting, about eight million had died. Families lost sons and husbands, fathers and brothers. Entire towns and villages lost their menfolk. Life was never the same again.

For the United States, separated from Europe by a vast ocean, the war was not nearly as devastating. It did not enter the war until 1917, and American troops were only involved in fighting for eighteen months. The United States tried to avoid being provoked into action, but once it had declared war, Americans responded with all their might. An army was quickly assembled and equipped and then shipped overseas. At home, workers (many of them women) toiled for long hours in factories where they produced the ships, shells, weapons, and uniforms that would be sent to the soldiers.

How and why did the war begin? In 1914 the most powerful nations in Europe formed two alliances. One consisted of France,

As tensions mounted across the continent, Europeans geared up for war. This photograph from 1914 shows German infantrymen on maneuvers, practicing drills in preparation for battle.

Russia, and Great Britain (the Allies). On the other side were Germany, the Ottoman Empire, and Austria-Hungary (the Central Powers). Italy remained neutral until 1915, when it declared war on Austria-Hungary. In the early 1900s Great Britain and Germany were in a race for control of the seas. Both nations started massive shipbuilding programs. The ships were fitted with huge guns capable of blowing any other ship out of the water. The race for sea power increased tensions between these two major powers. Other factors increased the unease. France, a long-time rival of Germany, feared German military power. The French expected Great Britain, an ally, to fight Germany if that nation invaded neutral Belgium,

This British woman, at work in an armament factory, learned to manufacture weapons. Mobilizing for war meant that European nations needed to stockpile large quantities of artillery. When men left home to train as soldiers, women filled the jobs they left behind.

France's neighbor. None of these tensions actually started the war, however. The immediate cause lay to the southeast, in the Balkans, a region ruled by Austria-Hungary. Here was the powder keg that, once lit, would blow apart all of Europe.

In 1908 Austria-Hungary had annexed Bosnia and Herzegovina, a region of the Balkans, and made it a province of its empire. This action angered another Balkan state, Serbia, whose ally was Russia. Both Austria-Hungary and Russia saw in the Balkans a place to advance their long-range plans. Austria-Hungary hoped to extend the borders of its empire south to the Dardanelles, the narrow body of water that connects the Aegean and Black Seas. Russia had long wanted control of the Dardanelles because it was a warm-water route for Russian trade. For its part, Serbia wanted to enfold Bosnia and other Slavic states into an enlarged Serbia. Such an action was likely to anger Austria-Hungary. Tensions in the region were great, but war was still avoidable when, on June 28, 1914, Archduke Franz Ferdinand of Austria-Hungary was assassinated by a Bosnian Serb nationalist in Sarajevo, the capital of Bosnia.

Now the diplomats of each nation sent threats (called ultimatums) to the other. The ruler of Germany, Kaiser Wilhelm II, immediately promised to come to the aid of Austria-Hungary if it decided to punish Serbia. When Serbia received the Austrian ultimatum, it began to mobilize, or prepare, for war. Great Britain meanwhile tried to keep the peace. On July 28 Austria-Hungary declared war on Serbia. Two days later Russia began to prepare for war, and one day later Germany and Russia were at war. On August 1, France began to mobilize on its border with Germany. Germany followed by mobilizing on its border with France. On August 2,

Italy declared itself neutral. That left only Great Britain to decide which route to take. Would the British stand behind their allies—France and Russia—or remain neutral? The deciding factor was whether Germany would respect the neutrality of Belgium, a small country that stood between Germany and France.

Germany's generals had a grand plan: to quickly invade France to the west, knock it out of the war, and then turn their army on Russia to the east. The quickest route to northern France was through low-lying Belgium. Years earlier, Germany—along with Great Britain and the other powers—had agreed to respect Belgium's neutral status. Now, Germany demanded that its army be allowed to march through neutral Belgium. Great Britain rejected the demand and asked that Germany stop its plans to invade. When the German leaders refused, Great Britain declared war on Germany. The date was August 4, 1914.

While the leaders of the European powers promised their soldiers that the war would be short, the American president had other concerns. President Woodrow Wilson, former president of Princeton University and governor of New Jersey, urged Americans (many of whom were of German ancestry or even recent immigrants from Germany) not to take sides. He also proclaimed that the United States was neutral.

Germany's subsequent invasion of Belgium and rapid advance on France caught the Allies by surprise. German forces moved in on Paris, and the French army fell back in retreat. Then, in September, the French saw an opportunity to attack the German advance. In several fierce battles, beginning with the Battle of the Marne, French and German armies battled each other to a draw. The German plan

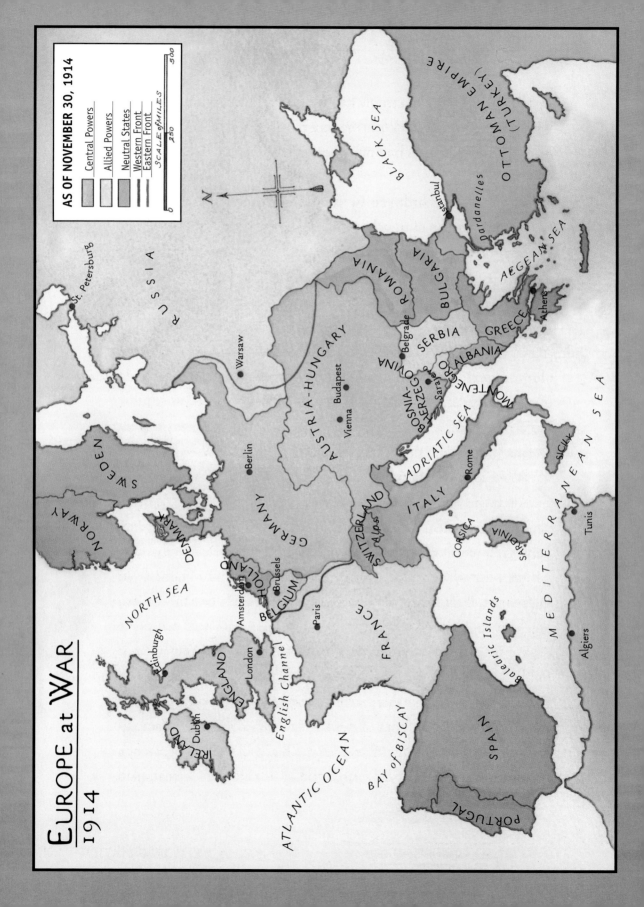

EUROPE at WAR
1914

AS OF NOVEMBER 30, 1914

	Central Powers
	Allied Powers
	Neutral States
	Western Front
	Eastern Front

SCALE of MILES
0 250 500

N

RUSSIA

St. Petersburg

Warsaw

SWEDEN

NORWAY

DENMARK

NORTH SEA

GERMANY

Berlin

HOLLAND

Amsterdam

Brussels

BELGIUM

London

ENGLAND

Edinburgh

IRELAND

Dublin

English Channel

ATLANTIC OCEAN

BAY of BISCAY

FRANCE

Paris

SWITZERLAND

Alps

AUSTRIA-HUNGARY

Vienna

Budapest

ROMANIA

Belgrade

SERBIA

BOSNIA-HERZEGOVINA

Sarajevo

MONTENEGRO

ALBANIA

BULGARIA

GREECE

Athens

AEGEAN SEA

OTTOMAN EMPIRE (TURKEY)

Istanbul

Dardanelles

BLACK SEA

ADRIATIC SEA

ITALY

Rome

CORSICA

SARDINIA

Balearic Islands

MEDITERRANEAN SEA

SICILY

SPAIN

PORTUGAL

Tunis

Algiers

to crush the French in a single hammer blow failed, but neither side was able to completely defeat the other. By the end of the year, German and Allied troops had dug themselves in along France's northern boundary.

To escape bombardment by the enemy's heavy guns, each army constructed a series of trenches that snaked back and forth for about 400 miles from the North Sea south through western Belgium and then across France to the border of Switzerland. This became known as the Western Front. It was impossible to go around the system of trenches; the only tactic was for an army to make a complete frontal assault against the dug-in enemy. Both forces used this tactic to try to break through the other's defenses. The results were terrible. Millions of soldiers were cut down in their tracks by machine-gun fire or exploding shells as they scrambled out of their protective trenches and moved across open fields. Hidden explosives and barbed wire made the contested territory a "no-man's-land." The war settled into a stalemate. Neither side was able to knock its enemy out of the fight.

On the Eastern Front, poorly prepared Russian soldiers were massacred as they attacked German forces across open fields. In Turkey, Australian and New Zealander soldiers of the Allied force unsuccessfully fought the Turks for control of the Dardanelles and access to the Black Sea. In the spring of 1915, Italy declared war on its former ally, Austria-Hungary. At sea Great Britain was using its navy to blockade, or cut off, all shipments of food and war supplies to Germany. In response, Germany declared a sea war against British and Allied ships. The ships of neutral nations (suspected of secretly carrying supplies for the Allies) were also targeted by Germany's most powerful weapon, the submarine. When submarines harassed

The *Lusitania* set sail for Europe on May 1, 1915. Six days later, a German submarine torpedoed the passenger ship, killing 128 Americans. With this tragedy, the United States found itself a step closer to declaring war.

American merchant ships, Americans began to call for a response. On May 7, 1915, a German submarine sank a British passenger ship, the *Lusitania*. One hundred and twenty-eight Americans lost their lives. Despite public outrage over the *Lusitania* tragedy, President Wilson was determined to keep America neutral. In the election of 1916, he ran for reelection on the slogan "He kept us out of war."

Nonetheless, the year 1917 saw America's entry into World War I. In January President Wilson called for "peace without victory" in a speech before the United States Senate. A few days later, the German kaiser called for unrestricted submarine warfare. This announcement spurred President Wilson to cut off all diplomatic relations with Germany, a step just short of a declaration of war. The same month, the British informed Wilson of the contents of the Zimmermann telegram. The note revealed a German plot to involve Mexico in a war against the United States. Irate Americans called for war. In March German submarines torpedoed three American ships. Wilson knew that any chance of keeping the nation out of the war had been lost. On April 2, 1917, he asked Congress to declare war against Germany; four days later, the United States was at war.

The American Expeditionary Force (AEF) was the name given to the American forces in World War I. Its leader was General John J. Pershing. The first American troops arrived in France on June 24, 1917, and paraded in the streets of Paris ten days later. The Americans arrived at the time when the French forces were at their lowest point. Exhausted by years of trench warfare, French soldiers refused to attack the enemy. British troops were equally worn-out. In contrast, the Americans were fresh and ready to fight. Soon they were tested in battle.

In June 1918 German forces smashed through the Allied lines on the Western Front and threatened to seize Paris. Doughboys (a nickname for U.S. Army soldiers) and Marines were rushed forward to stop the advance and met German forces near Belleau Wood. The Marines (whom the Germans nicknamed "Devil Dogs") boldly vowed to hold the ground at all cost. And they did just that. After the battle was over, the German advance had been checked, and Americans had earned the admiration of friend and foe alike. Other key battles followed. The Americans held their ground at Château-Thierry and attacked at St. Mihiel. In the rugged Argonne Forest, American soldiers clawed and crawled through a wilderness studded with German machine-gun nests. The doughboys called the area the "meatgrinder." The outnumbered Americans fought off the Germans and eventually drove them from the Argonne.

The vigor of American soldiers in combat proved to Germany that the war would continue for some time. Eventually, the Americans would overwhelm Germany's weary army. In early October 1918, the German leaders requested an armistice, that is, an end to fighting on land, by sea, and in the air. One month later, the kaiser, faced with rising discontent at home and the collapse of his armies, abdicated, or gave up the throne. Meanwhile the Allies were closing in on all fronts. In the Middle East, the British were on the verge of defeating the Ottoman Turks, an ally of Germany. On the Western Front, the British, French, and Americans were smashing through German lines. On November 10 a republic was declared in Germany, and one day later, on November 11, the Germans signed the armistice in a railway car in a forest outside of Paris. The Great War, as World War I was called, had come to an end.

What had the war accomplished? Four empires—Germany, Austria-Hungary, Russia, and Ottoman—ceased to be. Great Britain had lost a million men; France, 1.7 million; Germany, 2 million; Russia, 1.7 million; and Austria-Hungary, 1.5 million. American losses—about 120,000—were small in comparison, but large for the short period of time the AEF was in combat. One writer estimated that more men died in a week's fighting in the Argonne Forest than in the entire American Revolution. In addition to the huge number of dead, many soldiers returned home without legs or arms. Those who had been gassed never recovered their health. Others were mentally wounded, victims of "shell shock," or battle fatigue. To add to the already terrible losses of the war, a worldwide outbreak of influenza in 1918 killed between 20 to 40 million people. The most vulnerable were young men and women—the very persons most involved in fighting and supporting the war.

When the delegates of the Allies met in Versailles, France, in 1919 to discuss the terms of peace, they were a divided group. One

President Wilson *(right)* makes his way to the Versailles Peace Conference in 1919, along with the British and French prime ministers. Wilson hoped to craft a treaty that would promote world peace. But the people of Europe could not forget the devastation of the war years. To them, the treaty was a means to punish Germany.

year earlier President Wilson had presented his plan for world peace called the Fourteen Points. Some of the points he proposed included a reduction in the number of war weapons a nation could have and the right of all nations to govern themselves. He also wanted to establish an international organization (which he called the League of Nations) that would keep the peace and prevent future wars. But at Versailles in 1919 Britain and France were more interested in punishing Germany. When the peace treaty was signed in June of that year, Germany lost all of its overseas possessions and some of its territory. The treaty required it to reduce its once-mighty army to 100,000 men. Worst of all, Germany was forced to pay for all of the civilian damage caused during the war. The reaction in Germany was one of outrage. In time, resentment over the harsh terms of the peace treaty, coupled with economic hardship, would give rise to extremist political groups. By the 1930s, these new political groups would lead Germany into another war.

In the United States, people were happy to see the return of peace. Many said that the country should never again become involved in the affairs of other nations. They preached this philosophy of isolationism despite President Wilson's plea that the United States not turn its back on world affairs. In Congress, opponents of the president rejected his idea for the League of Nations. They also refused to sign the Treaty of Versailles. When Wilson left office in 1920, his health was ruined and his ideas about building a new world were largely cast aside. Nevertheless, the United States emerged from the war as a world leader.

In the following pages you will encounter many different primary sources. Each one deals with American involvement in World War I. Each contains the unique voice of an American leader, soldier, or civilian—men and women alike—who lived in the early 1900s and who experienced the war on the field of battle or at home.

The Krupp steelworks in the city of Essen, shown in this 1914 photograph, was the chief supplier of arms to the German Empire. Europe had been in a state of unrest for years before the start of the Great War. The continent's major powers had been amassing weapons, fortifying their armies, and forming alliances. By 1914, war seemed inevitable.

Chapter I

1914—Outbreak of War in Europe Sparks Reaction in America

WORLD WAR I BROKE OUT in the summer of 1914 after months of simmering tensions among the major powers of Europe. No one thought the war would last for long. National leaders hoped to achieve decisive victories in time to bring the soldiers home by Christmas. It was not to be. The war did not end by Christmas of 1914. Instead, it dragged on for four long years. During most of that time, soldiers lined up in trenches that stretched across the landscape of northern France all the way south to the Swiss border. There they sat and waited for their commander's order to advance against the opposing army's lines. These attacks turned out to be mass slaughters as men marched into a rain of bullets, machine-gun fire, and the explosions of thousands of shells. Poison gas, a new weapon, disabled soldiers and caused long-term suffering among survivors. This was war as never fought or experienced before.

Americans kept informed of the war primarily through newspaper articles and the numerous accounts of correspondents reporting from the front. Several of these accounts are included in the following chapter.

An Observer Delivers a Warning to President Wilson

President Wilson's closest adviser, Colonel Edward House, traveled to Europe in the spring of 1914 to observe the tensions between the major European powers. The following excerpt is from House's letter to Wilson. It was written in May of 1914. The outbreak of war was just a few months away, brought about in part by the competition among the major powers to build bigger and better-armed armies and navies.

THE SITUATION IS EXTRAORDINARY. It is militarism run stark mad. Unless someone acting for you can bring about a different understanding, there is some day to be an awful cataclysm. No one in Europe can do it. There is too much hatred, too many jealousies. Whenever England consents, France and Russia will close in on Germany and Austria. England does not want Germany wholly crushed, for she would then have to reckon alone with her ancient enemy, Russia. But if Germany insists upon an ever increasing navy, then England will have no choice. The best chance for peace is an understanding between England and Germany in regard to naval armaments and yet there is some disadvantage to us by these two getting too close.

—*From Charles Seymour, editor,* The Intimate Papers of Colonel House. *Boston and New York: Houghton Mifflin, 1926.*

1. How would you describe the tone of Colonel House's letter? Was he hopeful or pessimistic regarding the future of peace?

2. Why, in House's opinion, was it impossible for the nations of Europe to stop militarism?

3. What does Colonel House mean by an "understanding" between England and Germany?

Death of an Archduke: An Eyewitness Account of the Killing of Archduke Franz Ferdinand

Archduke Franz Ferdinand, nephew of the emperor of Austria-Hungary and heir to the Austro-Hungarian throne, was assassinated in the Bosnian city of Sarajevo on June 28, 1914. The assassin was a Bosnian Serb nationalist named Gavrilo Princip. This event was the spark that ignited World War I. The following is an account of the killing as witnessed by one of Princip's fellow terrorists, Borijove Jevtic. Both Princip and Jevtic were members of a secret society devoted to Serbian independence. Jevtic's account appeared in numerous newspapers, including the *New York World*.

When Francis Ferdinand and his retinue drove from the [train] station they were allowed to pass the first two conspirators. The motor cars were driving too fast to make an attempt feasible and in the crowd were many Serbians; throwing a grenade would have killed many innocent people. When the car passed Gabrinovic [another terrorist] . . . threw his grenade. It hit the side of the car, but Francis Ferdinand threw himself back and was uninjured. Several officers riding in his attendance were injured. The cars sped to the Town Hall and the rest of the conspirators did not interfere with them. After the reception in the Town Hall General Potiorek, the Austrian Commander, pleaded with Francis Ferdinand to leave the city, as it was seething with rebellion. The Archduke was persuaded to drive the shortest way out of the city and to go quickly. The road to the maneuvers [an army practice to be witnessed by the Archduke] was shaped like the letter V, making a sharp turn at the bridge over the River Milgacka. Francis Ferdinand's car could go fast enough until it reached this spot but here it was forced to slow down for the turn. Here Princip had taken his stand.

"As the car came abreast he stepped forward from the curb, drew his automatic pistol from his coat and fired two shots."

As the car came abreast he stepped forward from the curb, drew his automatic pistol from his coat and fired two shots. The first struck the wife of the Archduke, the Archduchess Sofia, in the abdomen. She was an expectant mother. She died instantly. The second bullet struck the Archduke close to the heart. He uttered only one word, "Sofia"—a call to his stricken wife. Then his head fell back and he collapsed. He died almost instantly. The officers seized Princip. They beat him over the head with the flat of their swords. They knocked him down, they kicked him . . . all but killed him. The next day they put chains on Princip's feet, which he wore till his death.

—From the New York World, *June 29, 1914.*

THINK ABOUT THIS

1. How does this newspaper account answer the questions who, what, where, when, and why?

2. After reading this account, do you think the assassination of Franz Ferdinand could have been prevented? Why? Why not?

A Reporter Witnesses the German Army's March into Belgium

Richard Harding Davis was a famous American war correspondent. Wherever there was a conflict, Davis was sure to be there to tell the story. Davis began his career in 1886 as a reporter for the *Philadelphia Record*. During the Spanish-American War, he rode with Theodore Roosevelt and his Rough Riders. His vivid writing style brought him many assignments but was not limited to reporting the news. Davis was also a noted author of short stories and novels.

With the outbreak of war in August 1914, Richard Harding Davis was in Belgium where he witnessed the German invasion of that neutral nation. The following excerpt is from Davis's eyewitness account of the German entrance into Brussels, the Belgian capital. In journalism, these accounts are called dispatches.

AT THE SIGHT OF THE FIRST FEW regiments of the enemy we were thrilled with interest. After for three hours they had passed in one unbroken steel-gray column we were bored. But when hour after hour passed and there was no halt, no breathing time . . . the thing became uncanny, inhuman. It held the mystery and menace of fog rolling toward you across the sea.

The gray of the uniforms worn by both officers and men helped this air of mystery. Only the sharpest eye could detect among the thousands that passed the slightest difference. All moved under a cloak of invisibility. That it [the color gray] was selected to clothe and disguise the German when he fights is typical of the German staff in striving for efficiency to leave nothing to chance, to neglect no detail. After you have seen this . . . uniform . . . you are convinced that for the German soldier it is his strongest weapon. Even the most expert marksman cannot hit

Thousands of German soldiers marched through Belgium on August 4, 1914, on route to attack France. Germany's decision to violate Belgian neutrality marked the point of no return, ensuring that Great Britain would enter the war.

a target he cannot see. It is a gray green. . . . the gray of the hour just before daybreak, the gray of unpolished steel, of mist among green trees. In comparison the yellow khaki of our own American army is about as invisible as the flag of Spain [red and gold].

"The men of the infantry sang 'Fatherland, My Fatherland.' Between each line of song they took three steps."

I have followed in campaigns six armies, but excepting not even our own, the Japanese, or the British, I have not seen one so thoroughly equipped. I am not speaking of the fighting qualities of any army, only of the equipment and organization. The German army moved into this city as smoothly and as compactly as an Empire State Express [a passenger train in the United States].

The infantry came in files of five, two hundred men to each company; the Lancers in columns of four with not a pennant missing. The quick firing guns and fieldpieces were an hour at a time in passing. . . . The men of the infantry sang "Fatherland, My Fatherland." Between each line of song they took three steps. At times two thousand men were singing together in absolute rhythm and beat. When the melody gave way the silence was broken only by the stamp of iron-shod boots, and then again the song rose. For seven hours the army passed in such solid columns that not once might a taxicab or trolley car pass through the city. Like a river of steel it flowed, gray and ghostlike.

—From Richard Harding Davis, dispatch to the News Chronicle, London, August 23, 1914.

THINK ABOUT THIS

1. How did Davis use words to paint a picture of the event he described?
2. What was Davis's impression of the Germany army?
3. In your view, what impact would this dispatch have had on readers in America?

A Description of the Burning of a Belgian City

Richard Harding Davis continued to report from German-occupied Belgium. In the following excerpt from a dispatch he filed in August 1914, Davis describes how the Germans set fire to the city of Louvain as punishment after supposedly being fired upon by Belgian snipers. Davis's story helped build support for the war among Americans despite the fact that President Wilson had declared the United States neutral.

LONDON, AUGUST 30—I left Brussels on Thursday afternoon and have just arrived in London. For two hours on Thursday night I was in what for six hundred years has been the city of Louvain. The Germans were burning it, and to hide their work kept us locked in the railroad carriages. But the story was written against the sky . . . and we could read it in the faces of women and children being led to concentration camps and of citizens on their way to be shot.

The reason . . . as given to me on Thursday morning by General von Lutwitz, military governor of Brussels, was this: on Wednesday while the German military commander of the troops of Louvain was at the

REMEMBER ·BELGIUM·

Buy Bonds
Fourth
Liberty
Loan

Hotel de Ville [city hall] talking to the Burgomaster [mayor], a son of the Burgomaster with an automatic pistol shot the chief of staff and German staff surgeons. Lutwitz claims this was the signal for the civil guard, in civilian clothes on roofs, to fire upon the German soldiers in the open square below. Fifty Germans were killed. . . . For that, said Lutwitz, Louvain must be wiped out. "The Hotel de Ville," he added, "was a beautiful building; it is a pity it must be destroyed."

"Remember Belgium": A poster stirs sympathy for the Belgian people, encouraging Americans to buy bonds. Proceeds from the bonds were used for "Liberty Loans"—money lent to the European nations doing battle against the Germans.

The city dates from the eleventh century, and the population was 42,000. The citizens were brewers, lacemakers, and manufacturers of ornaments for churches.

When by troop train we reached Louvain, the entire heart of the city was destroyed and fire had reached the Boulevard Tirlemont, which faces the railroad station. The night was windless, and the sparks rose in steady . . . pillars. In their work the soldiers were moving from the heart of the city to the outskirts, street by street, from house to house. In each building, so German soldiers told me, they began at the first floor, and when that was burning steadily passed to the one next. There were no exceptions—whether it was a store, chapel, or private residence it was destroyed. . . . in each deserted shop or house the furniture was piled, the torch was struck under it, and into the air went the savings of years, souvenirs of children, of parents, heirlooms that had passed from generation to generation.

The people had time only to fill a pillowcase and fly. Some were not so fortunate, and by thousands, like flocks of sheep, they were rounded up and marched through the night to concentration camps.

In other wars I have watched men on one hilltop . . . fire at men on another hill. . . . But in those fights there were no women and children, and the shells struck only vacant stretches of veldt or uninhabited mountainsides. At Louvain it was war upon the defenseless. . . . At Louvain that night the Germans were like men after an orgy.

—From Richard Harding Davis, dispatch to the New York Tribune, August 31, 1914.

THINK ABOUT THIS

1. In Davis's mind, what was the worst thing that happened at Louvain?
2. How do you think Davis got the information to write his dispatch?
3. What is the tone of Davis's writing in this selection? What do you think his intention was?

President Wilson in a speech to Congress urges Europe to settle its conflicts without further bloodshed. The American president tried hard to keep the United States neutral.

Chapter 2

America Is Neutral— At a Cost

PRESIDENT WOODROW WILSON tried desperately to keep the United States out of World War I. He knew the terrible cost the war would have on his fellow citizens. In an attempt to stop the conflict, Wilson asked the nations at war to state their aims, but neither side would do so. He even offered his own plan for a settlement in which there would be "peace without victory." Many Americans shared the president's reluctance to get involved. As they tried to understand the confusing causes leading up to the war, Americans became wary of foreign entanglements. Some citizens in the United States had no sympathy for the nations at war and their belligerence. Critics of the war thought it was just an opportunity for arms merchants and bankers to make money from the suffering of others.

For many Americans the war posed special problems. Many had divided loyalties. In 1917, America had a large immigrant population. One out of every three Americans was foreign born or had a foreign-born parent. Would these new Americans fight for their native lands or for their adopted country? In due time, each aggressive action by Germany filled Americans with growing outrage. They supported the victims of the war and wanted to help them. France, an American ally and the main continental power fighting against Germany, needed money and reinforcements for its battle-weary soldiers. Great Britain, France's ally, also needed loans and help in the form of food and war materials. The United States could not turn its back on their pleas.

Ultimately, the war at sea made it impossible for Americans to remain at peace. Germany's unrestricted submarine warfare against neutral ships (such as those of the United States) in the war zone around the British Isles swept American neutrality aside. As more American lives were lost, citizens realized the impossibility of staying out of the fight. In 1917, Woodrow Wilson sadly asked for a declaration of war between the United States and Germany and its allies. In a short time, American soldiers were at the front.

Danger on the High Seas: A German U-Boat Commander Describes an Attack on an Enemy Ship

When the war broke out in 1914, Great Britain, the world's leading sea power, tried to starve Germany into defeat by blocking off German ports. Ships of neutral nations such as the United States were stopped and searched for food or munitions or anything else that might help the enemy. Unable to block Britain's ports with its ships, Germany took another kind of action. It used submarines to wage war on its enemies.

Germany's use of the submarine (or U-boat, short for *untersee-boot,* the German word for submarine) marked the introduction of a new kind of warfare. Ships could be blown out of the water by torpedoes fired by an invisible enemy. In February 1915, Germany began unrestricted submarine warfare. It announced that waters around the British Isles were a war zone. Any neutral ships were exposed to danger if they entered the zone.

A submarine commander, Lieutenant Otto Weddigen, wrote the following account of U-9's attack on a British ship. During the course of one hour, U-9 attacked and sank three British cruisers.

IT WAS TEN MINUTES AFTER 6 on the morning of last Tuesday when I caught sight of one of the big cruisers of the enemy. I was then eighteen sea miles northwest of the Hook of Holland. I had then traveled considerably more than 200 miles from my base. . . . I had been going ahead partly submerged, with about five feet of my periscope showing. Almost immediately I caught sight of the first cruiser and two others. I submerged completely and laid my course so as to bring up in the center of the trio, which held a sort of triangular formation. I could see their gray-black sides riding high over the water.

When I first sighted them they were near enough for torpedo work, but I wanted to make my aim sure, so I went down and in on them. I had taken the position of the three ships before submerging, and I succeeded in getting another flash through my periscope before I began action. I soon reached what I regarded as a good shooting point.

"I soon reached what I regarded as a good shooting point. Then I loosed one of my torpedoes."

Then I loosed one of my torpedoes at the middle ship. I was then about twelve feet under water, and got the shot off in good shape. . . . I climbed to the surface to get a sight . . . and discovered that the shot had gone straight and true, striking the ship, which I later learned was the *Aboukir*. . . .

There were a fountain of water, a burst of smoke, a flash of fire, and part of the cruiser rose in the air. Then I heard a roar and felt reverberations sent through the water by the detonation. She had been broken apart, and sank in a few minutes.

—From Lieutenant Otto Weddigen, Commander of the U-9, The First Submarine Blow Is Struck. *Available on-line from the World War I Document Archive: http://www.lib.byu.edu/*

THINK ABOUT THIS

1. What skills did the U-boat commander use to destroy the enemy ships?
2. Soldiers and sailors have to report their actions to their commanders after an engagement like the one described here. What is the purpose of these reports?
3. Put yourself in the role of a sailor aboard a British or neutral ship. How would you feel about sailing into a war zone?

Torpedoes Strike! A Firsthand Account of a Torpedo Attack

On May 7, 1915, the British passenger liner *Lusitania* was torpedoed by a German submarine while traveling from New York to Liverpool, England. Although unarmed, the *Lusitania* was carrying cases of rifle ammunition and other war goods, apparently destined for the Allied armies. Nearly 1,200 passengers and crew died when the ship sank off the coast of Ireland. Among the dead were 128

An illustration from an English newspaper depicts the sinking of the *Lusitania* by a German submarine. The act killed 1,200 of the ship's 1,900 passengers, 128 of whom were American. The loss of American lives posed a serious threat to President Wilson's policy of neutrality.

Americans. In the United States and Great Britain, the public reacted with outrage as newspapers told the grim story. Other submarine attacks followed. Ship travel across the Atlantic became more and more dangerous.

The following excerpt describes the torpedoing of a British ship. It was written by Albert Kinross, an officer on board.

THE FIRST TORPEDO STRUCK US at a few minutes past ten o'clock in the morning. I was down below in the saloon with E. We had both kept a boat-watch during the night and were the last officers to come to breakfast. When the torpedo struck, there was no mistaking it for anything else. E and I laughed, as much to say: "Here she is!" Then I put on my cork belt . . . and leaped up the three flights of stairs that led to the liner's deck and my own boat station. E raced with me. I have never seen him since. The stewards and cooks raced with us too. There was something theatrical about that picture—so many white jackets and blue uniform trousers and white overalls. All this time—it might have been a couple of minutes—the greater part of me was so active that I have no recollection of any instant devoted to fear.

As one rushed upstairs one thought of things one had valued yesterday—two brand-new pairs of boots, one's field glasses, some money—they seemed now so utterly of no account. Providence must have been with me, for having arrived on deck, I stood flush before my boat, Number 13. I stood there and took charge. To [the] left of me the right people were busy with our sixty-six sisters. These ladies were part of the staff of a new hospital unit. Safely they were put into their boats, safely lowered, and safely rowed away from us. We cheered them as they left, and they cheered back.

"... suddenly her bow dropped, her stern lifted, and next she slid to the bottom like a diver. It was as though a living thing had disappeared beneath the waves."

I had filled my boat as full as it would go. All was ready. I stepped on board and gave the signal. Then slowly we descended. Above our heads one of the ship's officers was seeing to it that we went down all right. Immediately below us was another boat. It pushed off at last, and now we were free to hit the water. Before we pushed off I took on five of the crew who had helped to lower us. They swarmed down the ropes and reached us safely. Then I refused to take anybody else and we got oars and rowed away. Only then did I notice that the ship had stopped dead.

The big ship—she was near to 15,000 tons—stood like an island, and as if she could stand forever. Then . . . there was a flash and an explosion. A second torpedo had struck. . . . We noticed now that she had a definite list to starboard. The angle grew steeper, and then suddenly her bow dropped, her stern lifted, and next she slid to the bottom like a diver. It was as though a living thing had disappeared beneath the waves.

—From Albert Kinross, "Torpedoed," Atlantic Monthly, December 1917.

THINK ABOUT THIS

1. How did Kinross and his shipmate react when the torpedo struck?
2. Using the description of his actions as clues, what do you think Kinross's job was on board the ship?
3. How did Kinross describe the last moments of the ship? What in his description tells you how he felt?

President Wilson Speaks Out for Peace

"There is such a thing as a nation being so right it does not need to convince others by force that it is right."

The outbreak of war in Europe and submarine attacks on ships with Americans aboard led to heated debate in the United States about the nation's role. Some Americans wanted to remain neutral. They argued that the war did not involve America's interests. Others wanted the nation to join the war. In his speech of May 10, 1915, President Wilson expressed his feelings about America's role.

THE EXAMPLE OF AMERICA must be a special example. The example of America must be the example not merely of peace because it will not fight, but of peace because peace is the healing and elevating influence of the world and strife is not. . . . There is such a thing as a man being too proud to fight. There is such a thing as a nation being so right it does not need to convince others by force that it is right.

—From Address of the President of the United States at Convention Hall, Philadelphia, Pennsylvania, May 10, 1915.

THINK ABOUT THIS

1. What example did Wilson believe the United States should set?

2. What tone do you think the president was trying to achieve in this speech?

America on the Edge: The Zimmermann Note Reveals a Plot against the United States

On January 19, 1917, Arthur Zimmermann, Germany's foreign secretary, sent a telegram to the German ambassador in Mexico. In his note, Zimmermann proposed that Mexico and Germany unite in a war against the United States. The telegram was intercepted by British naval intelligence agents, who decoded it and released it to President Wilson. Wilson then had it released to the newspapers. The Zimmermann note greatly strengthened the position of those Americans who supported going to war with Germany.

BERLIN, JANUARY 19, 1917

On the first of February we intend to begin submarine warfare unrestricted. In spite of this, it is our intention to endeavor to keep neutral the United States of America.

If this attempt is not successful, we propose an alliance on the following basis with Mexico: That we shall make war together and together make peace. We shall give general financial support, and it is understood that Mexico is to reconquer the lost territory in New Mexico, Texas, and Arizona. The details are left to you for settlement.

You are instructed to inform the President of Mexico of the above in the greatest confidence as soon as it is certain that there will be an outbreak of war with the United States and suggest that the President of Mexico, on his own initiative, should communicate with Japan suggesting adherence at once to this plan; at the same time, offer to mediate between Germany and Japan.

Please call to the attention of the President of Mexico that the employment of ruthless submarine warfare now promises to compel England to make peace in a few months.

—From *Congressional Record, Vol. LVI, March 1, 1917, pt. I: pp.680–681.*

THINK ABOUT THIS

1. What did the German foreign secretary offer Mexico as a reward for its alliance with Germany against the United States?
2. How do you think Americans living in the southwest reacted to the contents of the Zimmermann note?

A World Safe for Democracy: President Wilson's War Message to Congress

In 1916, President Wilson demanded that Germany stop unrestricted submarine warfare. The Germans agreed to the president's demand and stated that they would not sink vessels without warning. One year later, however, Germany said it would resume attacking passenger and freight ships without warning. This action led to Wilson's

On April 6, 1917, newspapers across the United States announced the nation's entry into war.

call for war between Germany and the United States. The following are selections from Woodrow Wilson's War Message to Congress delivered on April 2, 1917. Four days later, Congress passed the War Resolution, which brought the United States into the war.

After his speech, Wilson commented to an aide, "My message of today was a message of death for our young men."

GENTLEMEN OF THE CONGRESS:

I have called the Congress into extraordinary session because there are serious . . . choices of policy to be made. . . .

Vessels of every kind, whatever their flag, their character, their cargo, their destination, their errand, have been ruthlessly sent to the bottom without warning and without thought of help or mercy for those on board, the vessels of friendly neutrals along with those of belligerents. Even hospital ships and ships carrying relief to the sorely bereaved and stricken people of Belgium . . . have been sunk with the same reckless lack of compassion or of principle. . . .

I am not now thinking of the loss of property involved. . . . Property can be paid for; the lives of peaceful and innocent people can not be. The present German submarine warfare against commerce is a warfare against mankind. . . .

With a profound sense of the solemn and even tragical character of the step I am taking . . . I advise that the Congress declare the recent course of the Imperial German Government to be in fact nothing less than war against the Government and people of the United States. . . .

We have no quarrel with the German people. We have no feeling towards them but one of sympathy and friendship. . . .

One of the things that has served to convince us that the Prussian autocracy was not and could never be our friend is that from the very outset of the present war it has filled our unsuspecting communities and even our offices of government with spies and set criminal intrigues . . . against our national unity. . . . Indeed it is now evident that its spies were here even before the war began. . . .

We are glad, now that we see the facts . . . to fight thus for the ultimate peace of the world and for the liberation of its peoples, the German peoples included: for the rights of nations great and small and the privilege of men everywhere to choose their way of life. . . . The world must be made safe for democracy.

—From Woodrow Wilson, War Message, *65th Congress, 1st Sess., Senate Doc. No. 5, Serial No. 7264 (Washington, DC, 1917; pp. 3–8).*

THINK ABOUT THIS

1. What, in Wilson's opinion, forced the United States to declare war against Germany?
2. What is the ultimate goal of the United States in entering the war, according to Wilson?

Chapter 3

Whose War Is It?

THE DECLARATION OF WAR did not end discussion about it. Some Americans were filled with dread at the thought of the huge sacrifices that lay ahead. Critics of the war—both government officials and citizens—spoke out against U.S. involvement. Some were pacifists; they opposed *all* war on moral grounds. Other critics viewed the conflict as being outside U.S. interests. People who took a firm stand against the war often suffered persecution for their beliefs. Some even went to jail for taking exception to U.S. war aims. Other Americans were anxious to end the war and saw their participation as the only way to bring it to a conclusion. They took patriotic pride in their willingness and ability to get the job done.

World War I saw the federal government mobilize for war in new and interesting ways. Special commissions such as the Committee on Public Information were set up to build patriotic support. Writers wrote stirring songs and artists painted vivid posters to capture the public's attention. Pamphlets were printed in several languages explaining America's role in the war. School textbooks

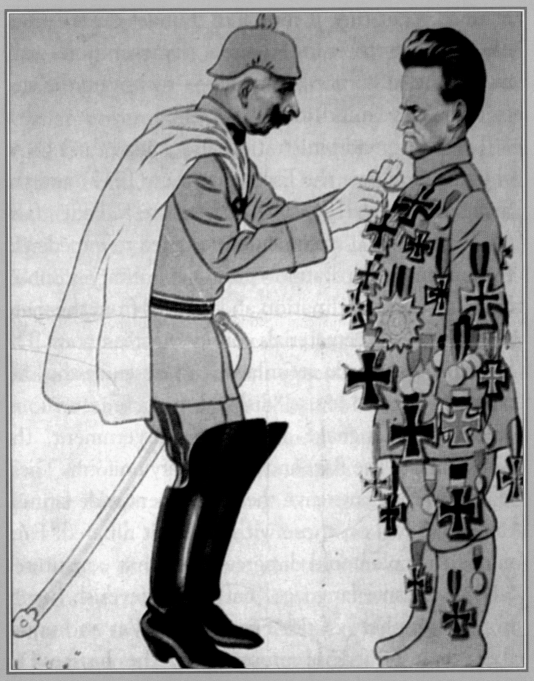

Cartoons published during World War I provide a satiric view of the times. This cartoon from *Life* magazine misrepresents Senator Robert La Follette as a traitor decorated with medals by the German Kaiser. For his part, La Follette believed that most Americans shared his opposition to the war: "The poor . . . who are the ones called upon to rot in the trenches, have no organized power."

urged children to help out, too. Everyone was asked to pitch in and "do their bit." American factories and workers churned out goods as never before.

An Opponent of the War Speaks Out: Senator Norris's Speech before the Senate

Not all Americans wanted the United States to enter the war. Pacifists spoke out against U.S. involvement. Peace organizations sprang up throughout the nation. Their members tried to influence congressional leaders and the newspapers. In Congress, opponents of the war included Senator Robert M. La Follette of Wisconsin and Senator George W. Norris of Nebraska. Both spoke out against the war and were bitterly criticized for it. The following excerpt is from Senator Norris's speech before the Senate, April 4, 1917, two days before the War Resolution was passed.

THE RESOLUTION NOW before the Senate is a declaration of war. Before taking this momentous step, and while standing on the brink of this terrible vortex, we ought to pause and . . . consider the terrible consequences of the step we are about to take. . . .

" . . . consider the terrible consequences of the step we are about to take."

The reason given by the President in asking Congress to declare war against Germany is that the German Government has declared certain war zones, within which, by the use of submarines, she sinks, without notice, American ships and destroys American lives. . . .

There are a great many American citizens who feel that we owe it as a duty to humanity to take part in the war. Many instances of cruelty and inhumanity can be found on both sides. Men are often biased in their judgment on account of their sympathy and their interests. To my mind, what we ought to have maintained from the beginning was the strictest neutrality. If we had done this, I do not believe we would have been on the verge of war at the present time.

It is now demanded that the American citizens shall be used as insurance policies to guarantee the safe delivery of munitions of war to belligerent nations. The enormous profits of munition manufacturers, stockbrokers, and bond dealers must be still further increased by our entrance into the war. This has brought us to the present moment, when Congress . . . is about to declare war and engulf our country in the greatest holocaust that the world has ever known.

—From Congressional Record, *65th Congress, 1st sess., Vol. LV, pt. I: pp. 212–213.*

THINK ABOUT THIS

1. According to Senator Norris, who would benefit by America's entrance into the war?
2. What action did Norris urge his fellow senators to take?
3. Did Norris present a convincing argument? Why or why not?

America Calls Forth an Army: A Citizen Explains His Opposition to the Draft

Once the United States was in the war, an army had to be assembled. On April 5, the government formally requested enforced service in the army. On June 5, 1917, ten million American men between the ages of twenty-one and thirty were required by the Selective Service Act to register their names with the government at local draft offices. In return, they received a green card with a number on it.

A recruitment poster encourages young American men to volunteer for military service. To ensure that the army had sufficient manpower, the government enacted the Selective Service Act.

The idea of a draft alarmed Americans. Immigrants, many of whom had fled enforced service in European armies, were especially upset by the new law. Opponents of conscription held protest meetings and asked that young men not register for the draft.

In the following excerpt from the *New York Herald,* Dr. Leonard Abbot, a speaker at an anticonscription meeting in New York City, gives his reason for opposing the law.

CONSCRIPTION IS IMMORAL, unAmerican, and unconstitutional. Why in the name of humanity drag us into a war which we disapprove? . . . Conscription is the thin entering wedge of military despotism. . . . Go to Europe and fight Germany if you want to, but do not try to drag us with you. . . . The Government must have a guilty conscience when it arrests college boys and girls and tries to break up meetings that are opposed to its conscription.

—From the New York Herald, *June 5, 1917. Quoted in H. C. Peterson and Gilbert C. Fite,* Opponents of War, 1917–1918. *Madison, WI: University of Wisconsin Press, 1957.*

1. On what grounds did the speaker oppose the draft?
2. What did the speaker fear the draft would lead to?
3. Think about writing a letter to the editor of the *New York Herald*. How would you present an argument for or against Dr. Abbot's statements?

A Song in Support of the War

Many government leaders believed the draft would result in mass riots across the United States. Much to their surprise, however, most American men went willingly to their draft offices. There they registered and were given a number. The number was thrown into a huge fish bowl and mixed up with others. Then the numbers were drawn out. The men whose numbers were drawn out were drafted into the army.

The call to arms was an opportunity for songwriters to express America's willingness to go to war. "Oh Johnny, Oh Johnny, Oh" was one of the most popular songs of World War I. The lyrics were written by Ed Rose to the music of Abe Olman.

This poster, designed especially to appeal to immigrants, asks Americans to support their nation and the cause of liberty.

Uncle Sam is calling now for ev'ry mother's son.
To go and get behind a gun,
And keep Old Glory waving on the sea.
Now prepare to be right there to help the cause along,
To ev'ry chap you meet when you're on the street,
You can sing this little song.

Oh, Johnny! Oh, Johnny! why do you lag?
Oh, Johnny, Oh, Johnny! Run to your flag.

Your country's calling, can't you hear?
Don't stay behind while others do all the fighting,
Oh, Johnny! Oh, Johnny! Get right in line
And help to crush the foe.
You're a big husky chap,
Uncle Sam's in a scrap,
You Go! Johnny,
Go! Johnny Go! Go!

—From "Oh Johnny, Oh Johnny, Oh!" written by Ed Rose. Music by Abe Olman.
Copyright 1917, renewed 1944, by Forster Music Publisher, Inc.,
Chicago, Illinois. All rights reserved.

THINK ABOUT THIS

1. To what emotions did the songwriters appeal in this song?

2. Why should American men fight, according to the words of "Oh Johnny"?

3. How would you have reacted to this song if you were a young man of draft age in 1917? How might you react today?

A Song of Protest against the War

"I Didn't Raise My Boy to Be a Soldier" was one of the most famous antiwar songs of World War I. It was written by Alfred Bryan and Al Piantadosi and came out in 1915. Pacifists and women's suffrage groups (those who supported giving women the right to vote) sang it at meetings to help attract followers to their cause. Of course, anyone who sang the song was suspected of being anti-American. Here is a chorus of the song:

> I didn't raise my boy to be a soldier,
> I raised him up to be my pride and joy,
> Who dares to place a musket on his shoulder,
> To shoot some other mother's darling boy?
> Let nations arbitrate their future troubles,
> It's time to lay the sword and gun away,
> There'd be no war today, If mothers all would say,
> "I didn't raise my boy to be a soldier."

—From "I Didn't Raise My Boy to Be a Soldier" written by Alfred Bryan and Al Piantadosi. Copyright 1915, renewed 1943 by Leo Feist, New York.

THINK ABOUT THIS

1. How did the songwriters think the war should be settled?
2. Who was the main audience for this song?
3. How would you have reacted to this song if you were a mother living in 1917? How would you have reacted if you were a supporter of the war?

Loyalty or Else! A Supporter of the War Recommends Harsh Treatment for Antiwar Americans

War showed that many Americans would not tolerate a difference of opinion. Dissenters were those who questioned U.S. involvement or opposed war on religious grounds. The press condemned dissenters as disloyal, and war protestors were often beaten by mobs. A common punishment was to force those suspected of disloyalty to kiss the American flag.

In the following excerpt from the *Sacramento Bee,* the writer expresses his opinion about what should happen to a teacher who questioned whether the United States was right in the war.

IT IS TIME FOR HER TO be put out of the public schools and to be put out forever. . . . And when another [teacher] declares she doesn't believe the Board of Education has the right to interfere with her religion and her conscience . . . then it is high time a drastic lesson be taught her . . . to the effect that the religion of Liberty and the conscience of the United States are above her creed and her opinion, and that she will have to obey!

—From the *Sacramento Bee, November 12, 1917. Quoted in H. C. Peterson and Gilbert C. Fite,* Opponents of War 1917–1918. *Madison, WI: University of Wisconsin Press, 1957, p. 112.*

THINK ABOUT THIS

1. Which rights were discussed in this excerpt?
2. Why would the opinions of schoolteachers be important to a nation at war?

The United States Takes Drastic Steps to Protect Itself: The Sedition Act

Once at war, the U.S. government took drastic steps against those who might harm the nation's war effort. The Sedition Act (May 16, 1918) temporarily suspended freedom of the press and freedom of speech. Both freedoms are guaranteed in the Bill of Rights of the Constitution. The Sedition Act was an amendment to the Espionage Act (June 15, 1917). The following is an excerpt from Section 3 of the Sedition Act.

WHOEVER, WHEN THE UNITED STATES is at war, shall willfully make or convey false reports or false statements with intent to interfere with the operation or success of the military or naval forces of the United States, or to promote the success of its enemies . . . or incite insubordination, disloyalty, mutiny, or refusal of duty . . . or shall willfully obstruct . . . the recruiting or enlistment service of the United States, or . . . shall willfully utter, print, write, or publish any disloyal, profane, scurrilous, or abusive language about the form of government of the United States . . . or shall willfully display the flag of any foreign enemy, or shall willfully . . . urge, incite, or advocate any curtailment of production . . . or advocate, teach, defend, or suggest the doing of any of the acts or things in this section enumerated and whoever shall by word or act support or favor the cause of any country with which the United States is at war . . . shall be punished by a fine of not more than $10,000 or imprisonment for not more than twenty years, or both.

—From Statutes at Large, *Washington, DC, 1918, Volume XL, pp. 553 ff.*

THINK ABOUT THIS

Do you think the U.S. government has the right to suspend the Constitution during wartime?

A private from the 69th Infantry bids his family an emotional farewell before departing on the long journey to the European war front. While some soldiers left their homes and families reluctantly, others set out looking for adventure and the chance to become heroes.

Chapter 4

Over There: Americans at the Front

THE AMERICANS SENT TO FRANCE in the summer of 1917 came from many walks of life and from many parts of the nation. Thrown together in training camps, young men forged new friendships that would last throughout the war. While some reluctantly took up arms, others looked upon the war as the experience of a lifetime and a chance to see the world. African Americans in particular saw the war as a means to advance their long struggle for equality—even if it meant dying in battle. "If this is our country, then this is our war," announced W. E. B. DuBois, the prominent African-American intellectual. DuBois wrote that "unstinting patriotism would lead to the right to vote and the right to work and the right to live without insult." Yet not all Americans favored allowing blacks in the armed services.

For most Americans, their arrival in France was their first encounter with another culture, another people, and another language. The war allowed them little time to appreciate these things, however. Young, inexperienced pilots, flying their delicate gossamer-winged planes, got their first taste of air combat with the best of

Germany's aces. Their deadly duels were fought above the chaos of the battlefields below. For the ordinary foot soldier, the war was far from glamorous. Those who survived would never forget the mud of the trenches, the terror of being bombarded day and night, the boredom of a soldier's routine, or the horror of combat. Men killed in the fighting never returned home; they were buried where they fell, with their brothers-in-arms in the fields of France.

Getting Ready: A Soldier Recalls Camp Life

Draftees into the U.S. Army came from all parts of the nation and from many different backgrounds. They were southerners and mid-westerners, city boys and farm boys. Some young men had college educations, while others could barely read and write. Regardless of where they came from and what they did before the war, the young men were about to become soldiers. Camps were set up around the country with the purpose of turning civilians into soldiers.

The following account is by Rex Thurston. In it, he recalls the time he spent at Camp Travis, Texas.

WHEN WE GOT OFF THE TRAIN, which stopped right in the camp, we were chased up to a barracks where we were examined for contagious diseases and also had a mouth examination. We were then taken up to dinner. It was about eleven o'clock. . . .

Each county was then separated and marched into the receiving station and waited until our county was called, and then fell into line as our names were called off. Each man was given a large envelope in which he placed all his money and valuables, and then sealed it. In

Soldiers at Camp Mead enjoy a well-deserved break. Young men from around the country traveled to military camps like this one, where they trained to become soldiers.

marching by a desk we delivered these envelopes to the party sitting there and he placed our name on it. We were then passed into a room where we stripped and wrapped our clothes in a paper. Our names were taken and placed on the packages. These are sent home by the government. From then on it was all action. We passed through a shower bath then went single file to doctor after doctor, a pasteboard around our necks and each one had something to write on it. Our finger prints were taken, all scars recorded and they began to hand out clothes. By the time a man gets around to shoes he is dressed from head to foot, and is also carrying a large bag full of clothes and blankets. We then sign up for everything, our pedigree is taken and we go on and are inoculated in the right arm and vaccinated on the left arm, and are marched out the front door dressed like soldiers but feeling a long way from being one.

Life in camp is full of surprises. We get up in the morning at 5:45 and must be dressed by 5:50, so you see a man has to make every move count. We then assemble in front of the barracks for reveille.

Breakfast at six. . . . At 6:45 we are called out for drill, which continues until 11:45. At twenty seconds before twelve the big siren on the fire station blows till twelve sharp and every soldier and officer in camp stands at attention. This is in honor of the boys who have fallen at the front.

"Life in camp is full of surprises."

Dinner at twelve-fifteen. . . . After dinner we attend lectures on army rules, articles of war, war material and everything pertaining to the army . . . at recess singing practice, and in spare times we clean our rifles which require a great deal of cleaning to pass inspection.

At 5:30 we are called out for retreat. This is when the flag is lowered. The roll is called, arms inspected and every man is supposed to be slicked up, shoes shined, clothes clean, and he must be shaved. This is one thing they insist on in the army—everything must be clean, barracks, porch and grounds.

—From Frank Freidel, Over There: The Story of America's First Great Overseas Crusade. *Boston: Little, Brown and Company, 1964.*

THINK ABOUT THIS

1. Describe the process by which the recruits were made into soldiers.

2. Why do you think the recruits' day was so tightly scheduled?

3. What does a person give up upon becoming a soldier? What does a person gain?

4. What do you think Rex Thurston thought of his training?

Foreigners in the Army: An Eyewitness Reports a Special Problem

Hundreds of thousands of southern and eastern Europeans came to America in the years just before World War I. When the United

States joined the war in 1917, these newcomers found themselves drafted into the army of their adopted nation. Strangers in a strange land, the foreign-born draftees quickly had to learn new ways. And the army had to find ways to teach the foreigners to be soldiers.

The following account is by Fred Rindge, secretary of the International Committee of the YMCA (Young Men's Christian Association).

I WENT TO THE GREAT cantonments expecting to see a great body of Americans. I found thousands of Italians, Poles, Russians, Rumanians, Greeks, and others—all potential Americans, to be sure, but with a long way to travel yet! In each of the several camps of 30,000 to 40,000 men I found 4,000 to 5,000 who understand little English and speak still less. . . .

"To build real soldiers out of this material is a slow process."

I talked with scores of colonels and other officers, and all agreed that this was one of their greatest problems. One regiment had about eighty percent "foreigners." Many had fifty percent. Whole companies were made up mostly of Poles or some other foreign nationality. Imagine these fellows from the slums of Chicago, Milwaukee, Detroit, Cleveland, New York, getting off their trains, being taken to camp . . . given instructions which they could little understand, and beginning . . . a life as new and strange to them as aeroplaning would be for you and me! . . .

To build real soldiers out of this material is a slow process, requiring infinite patience. One captain told me this as a joke on himself.

"Today when drilling my men I was provoked so many times by one fellow who refused to listen or obey orders that I sailed into him before the whole company. After I had completed what I thought was a rather impressive speech one of the non-commissioned officers saluted and said, 'Excuse me, Captain, but that man doesn't understand a word you're saying!' "

—*From Fred G. Rindge, Jr., "Uncle Sam's Adopted Nephews,"* Harper's Magazine, *July 1918.*

THINK ABOUT THIS

1. What was the army's main problem concerning the foreign-born recruits?
2. What did the writer mean when he referred to the recruits as "potential" Americans?
3. Why might a newcomer be opposed to fighting in the war? Why might he want to take part?

The Big Trip: A Soldier Writes about His Readiness for War

World War I became the experience of a lifetime for the soldiers who fought it. For most young Americans, the trip to France was the first time they had ever left their country. Here is what Sergeant Neil W. Kimball wrote in a letter from training camp before leaving for France and the war front.

"Every man knows the seriousness of the job he is going up against."

WE'RE ALL READY FOR THE BIG TRIP. All my possessions, a full equipment for fighting, eating, sleeping and even playing, is rolled up in a cumbersome roll of some eighty or ninety pounds, ready to be loaded on my back when the whistle blows. A year's training and we're ready to go in for the big thing—hear the cannons roar, but I know there is not a man in the outfit who would take a safe berth in the home guard, or even a discharge, if it was offered to him tonight. And yet, there is little of that "I'll bring back the Kaiser's helmet" stuff. Every man knows the seriousness of the job he is going up against, the filth and the dirt and the hardship they are going to bump into on the other side.

—*From Frank Freidel,* Over There: The Story of America's First Great Overseas Crusade. *Boston: Little, Brown and Company, 1964.*

THINK ABOUT THIS

1. How much training did Sergeant Kimball receive?
2. What did Kimball carry on his back?
3. Was the writer excited about his trip? Why or why not?

The Battle of St. Mihiel: A Diary Account of What It Was Like

By the time Americans entered the war, it had become a mind- and body-numbing round of raids and assaults on the enemy trenches. These assaults always followed the same pattern regardless of which side launched the attack. Before the light of day, the attacker's heavy guns would start a barrage of nonstop firing. Their fire was aimed at the guns and the trenches of the opposing army. The goal: to soften up the enemy. Then, at the sound of a whistle or a shout, the attacking soldiers would climb out of their trenches, hurdle across the lip of earth that protected them, and run, crawl, or zigzag

German soldiers sleep in a snowy trench as two stand guard. Fighting from the frontline trenches was grim and dangerous. It wasn't just enemy shell fire a soldier had to face, but also disease, hunger, bitter cold, rats, and lice. Sometimes men stood ankle- or even waist-deep in mud. Life in the trenches was miserable for soldiers on both sides of the war.

through an area covered with barbed wire, shell holes, and blasted tree stumps. During this mad dash through "no-man's-land," the enemy was firing with all its might. Few soldiers actually survived these assault waves. Most were cut down by machine-gun fire or exploding shells. If a trench was actually taken by the attacking soldiers, it was almost a sure bet that the enemy would get it back during the counter assault. This is the way the war was fought.

Corporal Elmer Sherwood was twenty years old in 1918. As a soldier in the 42nd Division (unofficially called the Rainbow Division) he served as a scout and telephone-line repairman. Sherwood took part in the Battle of St. Mihiel, one of the most famous World War I battles involving the American forces. Over four days in September 1918, the Americans captured territory that the Germans had held for four years. The victory was a great boost for America's spirit and proved to the Allies that U.S. soldiers could plan and carry out a big military undertaking.

Corporal Sherwood kept a diary during his time in the army. Here are his comments about his experiences in battle.

SEPTEMBER 12—The zero hour was 1:05 A.M., the heavy artillery starting it off. The earth seemed to give way when the rest of our guns joined in the stupendous and fierce barrage. The roar was so loud that we could scarcely distinguish the deep intonation of our own howitzers from the reports of the 75s.

For four hours the deafening roar continued as our messengers of death were hurled into enemy territory. Then at 5:00 our infantry preceded by tanks went over the top, making a picture of dash and activity.

The boys of our division leaped ahead of the clumsy tanks and pressed forward in irresistible waves to the German trenches.

The enemy artillery reply was feeble, though the infantry machine-gun and rifle fire was more menacing.

Our artillery fire in the first place demoralized enemy resistance, and the Boche [Germans] are surrendering in droves. Surely they must regret giving up these luxurious dugouts and trenches which they have lived in for four years. Many of them have electric lights and good furniture "requisitioned" [taken] from nearby French villages.

We must have slipped up on the enemy because they left a great deal of equipment, ammunition and food. Before we left the battery on detail work, two or three hundred prisoners passed our position. Up here in the advance we pass prisoners in droves of from ten to a hundred with a doughboy in the rear prodding the laggards with a bayonet whenever necessary.

A good many Germans are being utilized to carry back wounded. A sedate-looking officer wearing white gloves had to bow his back in the work just as his men did. It seemed to do these enemy enlisted men good to see their officers thus reduced to their own plane. Most of them became quite cheerful after they found that they weren't going to be scalped. . . .

"For four hours the deafening roar continued as our messengers of death were hurled into enemy territory."

The condition of the roads is very bad and No Man's Land is a mess of shellholes and mud. A good many enemy dead are lying about and a few of our men are lying where they were struck down by enemy fire this morning.

The doughboys are still advancing swiftly. In the air we are supreme. We are not in the position of the rat in the cage, as we were at Chateau-Thierry when enemy planes swooped down upon us and threw streams of machine-gun bullets into our ranks. This time the tables are turned. We see our aviators flying over the retreating enemy, dropping bombs and creating havoc.

—*From Elmer W. Sherwood,* Diary of a Rainbow Veteran, Written at the Front. *Terre Haute, IN: Moore-Langen Company, 1929.*

THINK ABOUT THIS

1. How did the battle begin, according to Sherwood's account?
2. What did the German soldiers think would happen to them at the hands of the Americans?
3. What kinds of details did Sherwood include in his account? Do you think they make what he had to say more believable? Why or why not?

The arrival of the Americans brought new hope to U.S. allies. Here grateful French villagers welcome two doughboys to their town.

African Americans in Battle: A Soldier Remembers

African Americans have always served in America's fighting forces. From the Revolutionary War to the Spanish-American War, black soldiers took up arms in the nation's defense. When the United States joined World War I, blacks were among those drafted into the armed services. The army was strictly segregated in 1917, however, and black draftees served in all-black regiments. One of the most famous of these all-black fighting units was the 15th New York. It eventually became the 369th Infantry Regiment of the 93rd Division. The 15th grew to 1,378 men and about 50 officers. Once in France, the men of the 369th Infantry spent nearly two hundred days on the front lines. The German soldiers called the men of the 369th the "Hell Fighters" because of their bravery in battle. The name stuck, and the infantry became known as the "Harlem Hell Fighters" in tribute to Harlem, a famous black neighborhood in New York City and the home of the 15th New York.

The following excerpt is from Haywood Butt's remembrance of

Officers from an all-black unit posed with a young French girl for this portrait. Nearly 400,000 African Americans served in World War I. African-American soldiers fought bravely for their country, struggling not only with war, but also with discrimination and the segregation policies of the day.

his days in the 369th. Butt was born in North Carolina in 1897 and moved to Harlem in 1912.

OUR UNIT STARTED IN 1913. There wasn't much to it at first. Boys used to drill with broomsticks up on 63rd Street, at St. Cyprian's Church. We drilled once a week in front of Lafayette Hall or on Seventh Avenue. The Boy Scouts gave us some military training. They showed us various soldier's positions. We didn't get any heavy combat training until we shipped out of the city up to Peekskill and Camp Whitman upstate. I was in the First Battalion of the 15th New York. In August 1917, when we shipped out of the city, we became the 369th. Pershing [the general in charge of American forces in Europe] wanted us to become laborers and to take our arms from us. That would have been sort of a disgrace, to disarm us. We went over to a New York regiment, and they didn't want us. None of the white units did, so we went around to the French. We fought side by side with the French. We were in five engagements. We fought in the Champagne [a region of France]. I was on the front lines for 191 straight days. I took the communique that apprised us of the armistice. I was relieved, because we were going over the top the next day. I daresay I wouldn't be here, because we were in Alsace [a region of France], and all of that terrain was mined. I didn't get back until February. We were taken to the Battery [the southern tip of Manhattan island], and people were waiting for us there. Our band, with James Reese Europe as the conductor, led us. We were the first ones to pass through that victory arch at Washington Square, then up Fifth Avenue. People were five or ten deep on the sidewalk, and they were throwing money down at us.

—From Jess Kisseloff, You Must Remember This: An Oral History of Manhattan from the 1890s to World War II. *New York: Schocken Books, 1989.*

1. How did Haywood Butt and the other men train at first?
2. What did Butt think of General Pershing? Why?
3. Why do you think the white units refused to join up with the 369th?
4. How were the African-American soldiers received when they returned home?

Forward or Die! The Men of the 369th Remembered

The 369th became famous for the bravery of its men and the dedication of its commanding officer, Colonel William Hayward. It fought in some of the bloodiest battles of the war—the Argonne Forest, Château-Thierry, and Belleau Wood. The 369th served as part of the 161st French Division. Because of its contribution to France the entire regiment was awarded the French Croix de Guerre, France's highest military honor.

This excerpt, from *Scott's Official History of the American Negro in the World War,* illustrates how the regiment gained its fame. Emmett Scott was special assistant for Negro affairs to the U.S. secretary of war.

THERE ARE MANY OUTSTANDING Exploits of the men of the 369th and of Col. Hayward himself. In Belleau Wood on June 6, 1918, the regiment came up to the German front lines where it met a very heavy counter-attack. Some one suggested that they turn back. "Turn back? I should say we won't. We are going through there or we don't come back," was what Colonel Hayward said as he tore off the eagles of his insignia, grabbed a gun from a soldier, and darted out ahead of the rest of Company "K," which went through a barrage of German artillery that was bearing down upon it. A French General ordered the regiment to retire, but Colonel Hayward, who, of course, was under direct command of this French General said: "I do not understand you." Then the French General raised his arms above his head and cried: "Retire! Retire!" And then Colonel Hayward with his hat knocked off, came running up and cried: "My men never retire. They go forward, or they die!" The regiment was cited eleven times for bravery in action.

"My men never retire. They go forward, or they die!"

—*From Emmett J. Scott,* Scott's Official History of the American Negro in the World War. *New York: Arno Press and the* New York Times, *1969.*

THINK ABOUT THIS

1. How did the American commander of the 369th react to the counterattack?
2. How did Hayward's reaction differ from the French commander's order?
3. What thoughts and feelings may have motivated Colonel Hayward?

Chapter 5

New Technologies Are Put to Use

WORLD WAR I WAS the first modern war. It was fought not just on land and at sea, but in the air as well. Deadly new weapons were developed and used by both sides. Soldiers were subjected to bombardment from massive guns mounted on railroad tracks, had bombs dropped on them from the air, and were suffocated by poisonous gases released over the ground. Tanks, armored vehicles of all kinds, airplanes, balloons, and submarines were just a few of the weapons of destruction that were used to some extent during the war. Despite these technical innovations, military leaders still followed old-fashioned battle tactics: stand-up assaults in which wave after wave of troops would march across a piece of land in an often futile attempt to seize the enemy's position. These assaults were mass slaughters. Most soldiers in World War I were killed by shrapnel from shells exploding around them. What shrapnel did not accomplish was carried out by bullets fired from rifles and machine guns. The amount of ammunition fired during World War I was so great that today's visitors to the battlefields still uncover shell casings—and even unexploded shells.

Before 1915, no soldier had ever faced the horrors of gas warfare. That year, the Germans recognized the potential of this new weapon. It could stun and confuse the enemy, making for a successful offensive. Soon chemicals were part of the arsenal on both sides of the war. Here U.S. soldiers struggle through a poisonous gas cloud. From 1916 to 1917, 17,000 soldiers died from the effects of these virulent weapons. Many more returned home from the war with permanent health problems.

Alarm! Gas! A Newspaper Account of a Poison-Gas Attack

World War I saw the introduction of chemical warfare. On April 22, 1915, German troops released gas containing chlorine over the Allied lines on the Western Front. The Allied troops were caught by complete surprise. The following newspaper accounts from the *New York Tribune* describe the gas attack and its effect.

NORTH OF FRANCE, APRIL 24.— ...The nature of the gasses ...remain[s] a mystery. Whatever gas it is, it spreads rapidly and remains close to the ground. It is believed not to be specially deadly—one that rather overpowers its victims and puts them *hors de combat* without killing many.

hors de combat
out of commission, unable to fight

BOULOGNE, APRIL 25.—The gaseous vapor which the Germans used against the French divisions near Ypres last Thursday . . . introduces a new element into warfare. The attack . . . was preceded by the rising of a cloud of vapor, greenish gray and iridescent. That vapor settled to the ground like a swamp mist and drifted toward the French trenches on a brisk wind. Its effect on the French was a violent nausea and faintness, followed by an utter collapse. . . .

The work of sending out the vapor was done from the advanced German trenches. Men garbed in dress resembling the harness of a [deep-sea] diver and armed with . . . generators about three feet high and connected with ordinary hose pipe turned the vapor loose towards the French lines. . . .

In addition to this, the Germans

"The attack ... was preceded by the rising of a cloud of vapor, greenish gray and iridescent. That vapor settled to the ground like a swamp mist and drifted toward the French trenches on a brisk wind."

appear to have fired ordinary explosive shells loaded with some chemical which . . . produced violent watering of the eyes, so that the men overcome . . . were practically blinded for some hours.

The effect of the noxious trench gas seems to be slow in wearing away. The men come out of their nausea in a state of utter collapse. Some of the rescued have already died from the aftereffects.

—*From the* New York Tribune, *April 25 and 27, 1915.*

<u>THINK ABOUT THIS</u>

How do you think the Allies reacted to Germany's use of poison gas?

Aerial Gunner: Arch Whitehouse Recalls His First Flight

The development of the airplane changed warfare. World War I was the first conflict in which the airplane was used as a weapon. When America joined the fight in 1917, it had just fifty-five outdated planes. America's Air Service was small compared with those of Great Britain, France, and Germany. Despite its unpreparedness and lack of well-trained pilots, the army Air Service proved its worth. By the end of the war, its pilots had brought down 755 enemy airplanes.

Before the United States entered the war, however, many adventurous Americans had already joined the conflict in Europe. They had gone to England and France in 1914 and enlisted in the army and air services of those countries. Arch Whitehouse was one of them. Arch was born in England in 1895 and moved to the United States in 1905. His family settled in Livingston, New Jersey. When

World War I broke out, Arch enlisted in the British armed services and was put to work grooming horses. This was not much fun for a young man seeking the thrill of combat. Before long, Arch discovered the Royal Flying Corps and transferred to a unit of battle planes. He learned to be an aerial gunner and eventually became a pilot. In later years, Arch Whitehouse became an author of numerous books on World War I. The following description is from his autobiography, *The Fledgling*, and describes Arch's introduction to flying.

THERE WAS A DULL RUMBLE outside and then the chug-chug-chug of an idling airplane engine. I sauntered to the door, opened it, and to my astonishment saw the wingtip of an airplane trembling not three feet from my front step. It seemed to be a gigantic biplane with four bamboo tail booms, a lot of struts and bracing wires. A great rumbling engine was set between the wings, and a flashing propeller whirled between the tail booms. The pilot clambered down and came striding toward my door, and I had to restrain an urge to slam it in his face. He had apparently taxied over from one of the hangars, but for what purpose I could not imagine. He was very tall, broad-shouldered, and ruggedly handsome. He smiled reassuringly, and under his unbuckled helmet I caught the glint of crisp, curly blond hair. He had a green scarf wound around his neck and wore a short leather coat, oil-stained boots, and murky whipcord breeches.

"You Whitehouse, the new gunner?" he cried cheerfully.

I had to think a second or two. "Yes, sir, but . . ."

"Good! Get your gear on. I'm going on an engine test. It'll be a chance to get your air legs in."

From his speech I judged he was either an American or a Canadian. But what on earth was he talking about?

"I've never been up, sir," I warned him.

"Fine. Nothing to unlearn. Just your helmet and goggles and that jacket. Loosen your puttees, circulation, you know." He squatted on the front step while I fumbled with the unfamiliar gear. "You're from the States, eh? I must say you don't speak like a Yank."

"New Jersey. That is, I volunteered from there, and I came through Canada. Worked my way over on a cattle boat."

" 'S truth! You sure were eager. I'm Clement—Captain Clement, Vancouver. You'll feel right at home in C Flight. Full of Yanks and Canadians.

"I'll take you up and show the balloon lines first, then we'll have a smack at a ground target. You'll enjoy that."

I had to be shown how to climb up over the undercarriage wheel, step carefully on the wing root, and wriggle my way up to the front

In the early days of aviation, airplanes were mainly used for sport, but the Great War would change this. Military strategists realized that airplanes could turn the tide of war, and aircraft of all kinds—from biplanes to blimps—were put to use. Here a gunner with the U.S. Flying Corps inspects his machine gun.

cockpit. This was the famous F.E. 2b pusher biplane of that day. . . . [I]t was known as the Fee. The pilot and gunner were accommodated in a light bathtublike body, or nacelle, mounted on the lower wing. The pilot sat with his back to the engine, and the gunner-observer huddled in a similar compartment out in front.

The gunner aboard the Fee had two .303-caliber Lewis guns. The first was mounted on a short length of gas pipe and pivoted on the floor of his shallow cockpit. This weapon could be fired through an arc of about 180 degrees. The second Lewis gun was bracketed on a crude telescopic mounting set between the pilot and the gunner. It could be brought into action against an enemy plane attacking from high in the rear. It *could,* if you pushed the mounting up as far as it would go and then climbed up and stood with your insteps on the upper edge of the plywood nacelle. From this precarious position, the gunner was expected to defend his tail—over the top wing.

Captain Clement was calmly explaining all this, while I was considering an immediate departure and wondering how I could renew old associations with the Yeomanry [Arch's previous outfit].

"It's simple," he said in much the same manner he would use to wish me a pleasant afternoon. "You can sit on the floor until we get up near the balloon line. After that, I want you to stand up, move about, and familiarize yourself with the gun mountings." He actually said that. He expected me to *stand up* in that three-ply canoe when we got into the air! The side of this aerial footbath hardly reached my kneecaps, and there was no safety belt.

"Now this flight is just to show you where our balloon lines are, which will be a help when we go to trench-strafing. You have to know whose trenches to strafe," he said pleasantly and moved the airplane out toward the center of the field. Now we were taking off, with a deafening roar of engine and propeller. We seemed to be speeding along at 1,000 miles an hour until we were clear of the ground; then I was certain that we were standing still or dangling from invisible wires. I huddled down deeper into my cockpit, hardly daring to move for fear I would tip the airplane over.

Scared? I was petrified. When the "enemy" started shooting at us, my pilot went into a daffy act, throwing our airplane all over the sky. There were great, greasy blobs of black smoke all around us, but did he head for home? He did not! He kept fooling around and actually tried flying through the antiaircraft smoke.

"He expected me to stand up in that three-ply canoe when we got into the air!"

Suddenly there was a loud pounding or banging somewhere behind. Well, we'd been asking for it. I knew we'd been hit—or that the propeller had slipped off and had cut our tail away. All that *could* happen aboard a Fee. My heart stopped.

What a letdown! It was just my pilot pounding on the metal space between us to attract my attention. Our tail was still out there on its four bamboo booms, and Captain Clement was grinning at me. ·

"Get up and take a look around," he yelled over the whine of the flying wires. . . . "[T]hen fire at the target. It'll be a white wing panel laid out on the ground. You stand up when I dive and fire over the nose. Then we'll go down and check your score."

"There it is," he yelled. "Get your gun ready."

The nose of the Fee tilted down at a dreadful angle, and I almost went out head first. No one had thought of safety belts for gunners. I clutched at the gun, shut my eyes, and tried to get my breath. I took another half-look and ducked to the bottom of the bathtub to await the end. Instead the floor of the nacelle came up and clouted me on the jaw, and my stomach tried to squeeze itself into those fluid ducts hollowed out of my spine. It seems that we had pulled out.

I learned all these snappy phrases later, but in the meantime we were zooming with a screech. I could see nothing but a pale blue sky. . . . and heard the pilot yelling, "Why didn't you fire? Let's try it again!"

I crawled around, and stuck my nose timidly over the edge, and spotted the target the Captain was so concerned about. From what I could make out, it was made up of three discarded wing panels laid out on the ground to represent the general outline of an airplane.

I began to have some idea of the game. . . . Clement curled the plane over in a tight turn, and I closed my eyes until I sensed that we had straightened out. When my intestines agreed to stay where they belonged, I knew we were flying reasonably level—and manfully took over my gun.

Down we went once more, and I think I kept my eyes open this time. I know I did *press* the trigger, and I *did* aim the gun; but how I put such a beautiful burst of forty-seven rounds into one of those panels was something only the gods decided.

We circled once more. Clement shut off the engine, and to my grim relief we landed safely beside the target.

"Holy smoke!" Captain Clement gasped. "They certainly train gunners in that Yeomanry outfit. Keep this up, young fellow, and you can fly with me any day."

We climbed back into the Fee and taxied across the field to the hangars. An armorer came out and removed the guns. "How many rounds did you fire?" he demanded in a surly tone.

"About fifty or so, from the front gun," I explained.

He spun the drum once or twice and peered inside. "There's been less than thirty fired from this drum," he argued.

I was glad that Captain Clement did not hear that. I could only assume that the target-keeper had forgotten to paste up the hits scored by a previous gunner. I probably hadn't hit the damn thing at all!

—From Arch Whitehouse, The Fledgling: An Autobiography. *New York: Duell, Sloan and Pearce, 1964.*

THINK ABOUT THIS

1. What was Arch's job on the airplane?
2. Did Arch look forward to his first flight? Why? Why not?
3. Why do you think Arch disliked Captain Clement at first?

An Incredible Escape: An Account of the Dangers of Flight

The use of airplanes by the Allies and Germany made World War I different from other wars. Dogfights—air battles between enemies—were fought over the Western Front, often within view of the soldiers on the ground. During these combats a pilot would try to disable the enemy airplane by firing at it with his guns. The goal was to force the enemy pilot to crash his airplane or withdraw from the fight. Sometimes a pilot would let his foe live if he showed fairness or unusual skill and daring in combat.

The war in the air sparked the American imagination. Aviators who succeeded in shooting down at least five enemy planes were called "aces." They became heroes of the press, and their deeds of daring became legendary.

A pilot's life was not all aerial warfare, however. Pilots also flew observation missions over enemy lines. The purpose of these missions was to observe the movements of the enemy. During these flights, the pilot was accompanied

World War I aviators who succeeded in shooting down five planes or more—like American Edward Rickenbacker shown here—were called aces. The greatest of all World War I aviators was not an American or an Ally, but German flying ace Manfred von Richthofen, better known as the Red Baron. He is credited with single-handedly shooting down eighty Allied planes.

by an observer-cameraman whose job was to take pictures of the battlefield below. Photography was thus united with aviation in the carrying out of war.

In the following excerpt, one pilot recalls a memorable flight in which his observer turned out to have all the luck.

THE MOST INCREDIBLE adventure came to Lieutenant Gardiner H. Fiske one day while he was flying as an observer in training maneuvers. The pilot, Lieutenant Samuel P. Mandell, wrote:

"I had the thrill of my life yesterday. We were flying formation in these great big busses [slang expression for an airplane] and the machine I had had two camera guns on it, one for the pilot and one for the observer. Old Fiske was standing up on the seat in back shooting away with his camera gun at a scout machine that was flying around us. At the same time I dove to get a shot at him with my gun. I heard a sort of a crash behind, and after I had straightened out looked around to see what it was. Lo and behold, a man in a leather coat was holding onto the tail of my machine. I could hardly believe my eyes, but Fiske had fallen out of his cockpit when his gun broke loose from its fastenings and I had nosed over. The first thought that came to me was: Will he have strength enough to hold on till I get down to the ground? I put the machine in the gentlest glide I could and started for home, as I could not land where I was up on the mountain-tops. . . . Fiske all this time was lying with his body across the fuselage right next to the vertical stabilizer on the tail. As I watched him over my shoulder, he gradually wound his way up the fuselage. He got a-straddle of it and gradually slid up . . .

> *"Lo and behold, a man in a leather coat was holding onto the tail of my machine. . . . Fiske had fallen out of his cockpit when his gun broke loose."*

and dove head first into his seat. About ten years' weight came off my shoulders by this time. . . .

Fiske today is reposing in bed, having been excused from all formations. He will never come any nearer death at the front, and nothing can ever scare me any more then this did."

—From Frank Freidel, Over There: The Story of America's First Great Overseas Crusade. *Boston: Little, Brown and Company, 1964.*

Think about This

1. What did the pilot do to try to save Fiske?
2. Which would you have preferred, to be a soldier in the trenches or a pilot in the sky? Why?

Tanks: A Description of a New Weapon

Tanks were among the new weapons that appeared in World War I. They were first used by the British Royal Tank Corps and later by the Americans. Plated with metal and fitted with belts in place of wheels, tanks were called "cross-country caterpillar vehicles" by Winston Churchill of the British Admiralty. They could go where animals and men could not. They could run down the enemy, travel over ground pocked with shell holes, and plow through barbed wire. Tanks had their drawbacks, though. They were clumsy, they often broke down, and they could be blown up by antitank mines. In World War I, tanks never replaced machine guns, cannon, or rifles.

Here is a description, which appeared in an article in the *Atlantic Monthly* magazine in 1917, of several kinds of tanks.

THE MARK IV TANK is a slow and sullen dinosaur. Four miles an hour is his limit. Frequently . . . he mounts a platform on his back and carries a sixty-pounder gun; or hauls a sledge, like an ox team, to pull big howitzers over shell craters. The Mark V is the next step upward in evolution. He is good for five miles an hour, has made nine, and one man can drive him. When I climbed down into the hot and whirring middle of a Mark V, heard the gears squeal and roar, and saw through the eye-slits the ground swinging under us, I knew how a steam roller might feel. . . . Nothing could stop our many ton, hundred and fifty horse power. We came to a trench, swung up, so easily, and down with scarcely a quiver, and so on about our business.

The Whippet . . . is light . . . and carried a cab like a camel's hump. The Whippet has two engines. As she runs her eight, ten . . . twenty

The tank, credited with saving many lives during World War I, was yet another weapon to make its first appearance during the Great War.

miles an hour, she squeals raucously. At a rock or stump . . . she whirls with unbelievable rapidity till your eyes are looking one way and your stomach another. She rumbles gaily over the field, sees a trench, rises on her hind quarters, drops below sky-line with a teeth-shaking bump, grips the further bank, rolls up screaming, and charges off for more. Never was devised a more dangerous . . . engine of warfare than this.

"Never was devised a more dangerous . . . engine of warfare than this."

—From Henry Seidel Canby, *"Education by Violence,"*
Atlantic Monthly, *1917.*

THINK ABOUT THIS

1. How does the writer use animal imagery to describe the tanks?

2. Do the tanks described in this excerpt sound terrifying or amusing?

3. Do you think the writer approves or disapproves of tanks as weapons of war? How can you tell?

A Red Cross ambulance, used at the front during World War I

Chapter 6

Civilians at the Front

AS WE HAVE SEEN, Americans were taking part in the war even before 1917. Some joined the armed services of France, Great Britain, or Canada at the start of the war because they wanted to help the Allied cause. These "Yanks" became valuable additions to the foreign forces and propagandists for American involvement in the fight. Civilians from all walks of life also threw themselves into helping out. Young college men from the United States traveled overseas to volunteer as ambulance drivers. They took on the dangerous job of shuttling wounded soldiers back from the front. Young college women went overseas to help out in any way they could. Some took jobs settling refugees displaced from their homes. Doctors and nurses from American hospitals volunteered to tend the wounded. Many more used their talents to raise money for the Allies. There was no end of war work for those who wanted to help.

The American Ambulance Field Service:
A Famous Poet Describes Its Work

John Masefield was an English poet and writer. He was born in 1878 and went to sea while still a boy. He traveled the world, often doing odd jobs and writing poetry. His best known poems, such as "Sea-Fever," are about the sea and seafaring men, but Masefield also wrote newspaper and magazine articles, military and naval histories, and children's books. During World War I, he went to France where he observed the war at close range.

Even before the United States joined the war, many Americans had decided to help France. Some helped people who had been driven from their homes by the war. Others volunteered to help transport wounded soldiers to hospitals. At first, the volunteer ambulance drivers provided their own cars. As the war dragged on, the ambulance of choice became the Model T Ford. Driving it was a challenge: the Model T was fitted with three foot pedals and a hand lever. In addition to operating the vehicle, the driver had to be able to repair it.

In the following excerpt from a magazine article, Masefield writes about the work of the American volunteer ambulance drivers.

AFTER SUPPER, in the last of the light, the ambulance-cars are made ready; the two drivers in each car put on their steel helmets and take their gas masks, and the convoy moves out, car by car, toward the Postes de Secours, where they will find the wounded. Some camps are so far from the front that the first part of the journey up can be done with headlights. All roads leading to the front are crowded with men or wagons going up or coming down. The image of this war will be of

Poste de Secours
first aid station

a convoy of many wagons, driven by tired men, going on and on along the darkness of a road . . . each man seeing no more of the war than the tail-board of the wagon in front.

As the car runs in the open, the drivers see the star-shells going up and up, and bursting into white stars, and pausing and drifting slowly down. . . . They are the most beautiful things in modern war and almost the most terrible. In this open space the drivers can see for some miles over the battlefield. As far as the eye can see, the lights are rising and falling. There is not much noise, but a sort of mutter of battle with explosions now and then. Perhaps ten miles away, there is fighting, for in that quarter the sky glimmers as though with summer lightning; the winks and flashes of the guns shake and die across the heaven.

Just overhead as the car passes comes a blasting, shattering crash which is like sudden death. Then another and another follow . . . right overhead. On the tail of each crash comes the crying of the shell, passing overhead like a screech-owl, till it is far away in the enemy lines, where it bursts. Above the engines one shell's noise is heard; the screech of its rush comes very near, there is a flash ahead, a burst, and the patter of falling fragments. Another shell bursts behind the car, and another on the road in front; the car goes around the new shell-hole and passes on.

This is "the front."

[The ambulance drivers arrive at the Poste de Secours.]

The drivers go down the sloping path into the cellars. Presently the sick arrive, haggard and white, but able to walk and the ambulances are free to go. The stretchers are passed into the ambulances, the sick are helped on to seats, they are covered with blankets, and the doors are closed. Shells from the enemy rush overhead and burst in a village which lies on the road home. They are strafing the village; the cars have a fair chance of being blown to pieces. The drivers start their engines and turn the cars for home; the rain drives in their faces as they go, and along the road in front of them the shells flash at intervals, lighting the tree-stumps.

These drivers are the very pick and flower of American life. The greater number of them young men on the threshold of life. All life lies before them in their own country, but they have …come to help France in her hour of need. All live a life of danger and risk death nightly.

—From John Masefield, "The Harvest of the Night," Harper's Magazine, May 1917.

THINK ABOUT THIS

1. How does the writer use words to paint a picture of the front?
2. Why is this piece called "The Harvest of the Night"? What is being harvested?
3. How do you think the writer was able to get to know the work of the ambulance drivers?

A Doctor at the Front: The Journal of Dr. Harvey Cushing

For the hundreds of thousands of soldiers who were killed outright in battle during World War I, scores more died of injuries or disease. Shrapnel from exploding shells killed or maimed countless soldiers. Poison gas burned the lungs and eyes. Foot infections led to the loss of toes and feet. Hours spent in muddy trenches resulted in deadly fevers. Army doctors saw wounds they had never seen before.

Dr. Harvey Cushing was a surgeon in World War I. Early in the war he served with a Harvard Unit in the American Ambulance (Hospital) in Paris. From there he went to Flanders (a region of western Belgium) where he worked with Britain's Royal Army Medical Corps. When the United States joined the war, Dr. Cushing was appointed a senior consultant to the Medical Headquarters

Caring for the sick and wounded was a harrowing experience for the doctors and nurses who came to help, leaving them with terrible memories of the suffering they had witnessed.

of the American Expeditionary Force. He saw firsthand the suffering of French, British, and American soldiers. During his time at the front—1915 to 1918—Dr. Cushing kept a journal of his experiences. Some of his observations are included here.

A DESCRIPTION OF "TRENCH FOOT"—

Many of the men have deformed toes . . . and they complain that their military shoes are bad. But there are other bizarre troubles with the men's feet of really serious nature. There are painful blue, cold, extremities; and indeed the whole circulatory condition of many of [the wounded] is very bad. The standing in cold water, even though above the freezing point—one cause of the so-called water-bite—is as bad as frostbite itself, especially when helped by the too-tight application of puttees which may shrink. Some of these poor devils must have so stood for days in hastily dug trenches without a chance of getting off their boots.

HOW THE WOUNDED ARE ORGANIZED—

At the Ambulance [the name of the military hospital outside of Paris], working on histories all the afternoon. Some of our recent cases have appeared tagged with pink cards which are tied on at a [first-aid station]. . . . I gather that there are two zones of these first-aid stations, primary and secondary, the wounded being gathered up from the battle-fields or trenches usually at night and taken to the primary line. There are several kinds of labels—pink (those capable of transportation), yellow, blue, and so forth. From the first-aid stations they are taken in peasants' carts or ambulances to an evacuation center which may be anywhere, preferably some railroad station, and there sitting and lying cases are separated, the serious from the minor cases, the medical from the surgical. The slightly wounded remain and before long go back to the Front; the bad cases—chest, abdomen, head, spine, and so forth—are sent to the nearest base hospitals.

KINDS OF WOUNDS—

The wounds in most cases of course are multiple. "Multiple" indeed may hardly convey the impression. Mostly shell explosion effects—very few bullet wounds. Indeed the more trifling the wound appears to be, the more serious it may prove on investigation. Or the reverse may be true—an ugly-looking wound that proved relatively trifling. One boy had a small temporal wound and stated that there was a hole in his tin hat. The operation showed that a strip of his helmet about two inches long and a half inch wide had been cut out as though by a can opener. This metal sliver had curled in through the temporal bone over his ear, passed through the brain, and its point emerged just behind the external angular process. Not a pleasant thing to dislodge. . . .

SOME AMAZING ESCAPES—

One comes upon many examples of hairbreadth escapes. In our wards is a man who got off with a slight burn of the forearm when a German contact shell exploded near him, and yet many of his companions were killed. Another man had both bones of his forearm broken in similar fashion without being actually hit, and yet his more distant companions suffered heavily from shrapnel. One man was blown into a tree and hung there for a long time by his trouser leg. Another was blown out of a trench and found the timing piece [fuse] of a shell in the seat of his trousers. Many have barely escaped because they happened to be stooping when a shell exploded near by. One artillery officer was knocked down three times in succession by shells landing only a metre or two away from him; he suffers from a severe nervous concussion—what the British call "shell shock."

ORIGIN OF THE WORD "BOCHE"—

This term of derision which we have heard our wounded at the Ambulance apply to the Germans—like Yanks and Rebs of the 60's [1860s, during the American Civil War]—I'm told is a contraction of "caboche"—a hobnail for shoes or the square head of a horseshoe nail—and has reference to the shape of the Teuton's head, which amuses the oval-faced and oval-headed Gaul.

USE OF MAGNETS IN HEAD SURGERY—

. . . after lunch another operation on the man we had X-rayed yesterday, disclosing a foreign body about 5 cm. in and forward in the cranial vault [skull]. . . . There were a lot of indriven bone fragments evidently infected, and at the bottom of the track the fragment of shell or whatever it was could be detected, but it would have taken a lot of manipulation with consequent damage to the brain to get it out. So we packed up and lugged the man down three flights to the first floor . . . and there I tried the famous magnet. I missed the fragment the first time and feared that after all it was lead and a piece of shrapnel ball—but on the second try, out it came, hanging to the end of the large probe.

THE BATTLEFIELD AFTER THE BATTLE—

. . . words fail to give any conception of the desolation. No convulsion of Nature could have done what man and man's machines have done. We bumped our way along a partly repaired road . . . passing craters from those 10 to those 30 feet across, and some almost as deep; passing rows and rows of old wire entanglements, communication trenches, line upon line of fighting trenches, all more or less obliterated. It was an upheaval of sandbags, broken rifles, tools, cartridge clips and machine-gun ribbons, food tins, water bottles, helmets, unexploded shells of every size, hand grenades, bits of clothing—and often smells, though two months have given ample time for burials. What may be in the bottom of the pits, however, one can only guess.

OPERATING UNDER FIRE—

TUESDAY, JULY 31—What may go down in history as the third battle of Ypres (July 31, 1917) opened to day. . . . After a week of favorable weather came the deluge.

AUGUST 1, 1:30 A.M.—Pitch black, pouring rain, and has been . . . nearly all this fearful day. Two ambulance trains, about a mile long, standing between the officers' quarters and the hospital encampment. The preoperative hut is still packed with untouched cases, so caked with mud that it's a task even to strip them and find out what they've got.

AUGUST 2, 2:30 A.M.—Pouring cats and dogs all day—also pouring cold and shivering wounded, covered with mud and blood. The preoperation room is still crowded—one can't possibly keep up with them; and the unsystematic way things are run drives one frantic. The news, too, is very bad. The greatest battle of history is floundering in a morass, and the guns have sunk even deeper than that.

10:30 P.M.—Operating again all day, and finished up an hour ago. A lot of wounded must have drowned in the mud. One of today's cases was a young Scot having attacks from a sniper's ball through his tin hat, a piece of which was driven into the brain. He had lain, he said, in the protection of a shell hole with one or two others—the water up to his waist—for twelve hours before they were found.

—*From Harvey Cushing,* From a Surgeon's Journal. 1915–1918. *Boston: Little, Brown, and Company, 1936.*

THINK ABOUT THIS

1. What happened to soldiers with only minor wounds?
2. What were some of the effects of being hit by shrapnel?
3. What nonmedical factors did the doctor have to deal with?
4. Why do you think a doctor would keep a journal of the war?

Women in the War: The Signal Corps Does Its Bit

Before World War I, there were no women in the regular army or navy. That changed in 1917. About 12,000 women served in the U.S. Naval Reserves from 1917 to the end of the war in 1918. The yeomanettes, as the women were called, worked as clerks, draftswomen, translators, camouflage designers, and recruiters—all jobs once held by men.

America's need for women workers extended into other areas as well. In 1917, the War Department called for telephone operators to serve in France. They had to be able to speak both English and French because they would be acting as interpreters between the French and American commanders. The women were carefully chosen for their skill and character. They would have knowledge of troop movements so their trustworthiness was of the utmost importance. More than seven thousand women applied to be members of the Signal Corps. About two hundred of these were selected and sent to Europe. The first unit of telephone operators was led by Grace Banker, a former instructor of the American Telephone and Telegraph Company.

Once in Europe, the women of the Signal Corps were nicknamed "Hello Girls." They served at U.S. Army headquarters in France and in towns in England and France. During the last

The women of the Signal Corps, who were required to speak both English and French, worked as telephone operators, facilitating communication between French and American commanders.

months of the war, the women operated communications equipment behind the front lines. The following is a recollection of a Signal Corps operator. She tells what it was like to bridge the gap between American and French ways of communication during World War I.

MOST OF OUR TOLL CALLS had to go over the French lines, and that sometimes made things very trying. When you wished to call over the French line, you said, "J'ecoute." ("I listen.") After a quarter of an hour, the conversation would begin with an exchange of pleasantries. "Good morning, how are you? Are you tired today. If you please, I should like to get_____ [a certain town]." All this had to be in honeyed tones, otherwise there wasn't the slightest chance of getting any attention. And mademoiselle would reply, "Ah, oui," in a languid sort of way, as if the call were of no particular moment, but might as well be handled, now that she was about it. If you asked for one place too often, you committed a serious blunder, for the result would be something like this: "You are unbearable, you ring too much, it gets on my nerves. Je coupe! (I disconnect)" and—bing, the line would be lost and that was an end to that.

—From Lettie Gavin, American Women in World War I: They Also Served. Niwot, CO: University Press of Colorado, 1997.

THINK ABOUT THIS

1. The writer described the way she dealt with the French operator. What did she have to do to get her attention?

2. Why was the work of the telephone operators so important during the war?

Nurses in France serve soldiers at an American Red Cross canteen.

Women in the War: The Nurses— A Remembrance by Eva Belle Babcock

The need for doctors and nurses during World War I was great, and many American health-care workers answered the call. Volunteer nurses were attached to the Army Nurse Corps. It was headed by Julia Catherine Stimson. Near the front, nurses set up mobile tent hospitals to receive the wounded. They cleaned the wounded, took part in operations, and gave comfort to the dying. Sometimes the women worked 40 and 50 hours without rest. Once their work was done, the nurses took the tent hospital down and moved to the next area of need.

Eva Belle Babcock was one of the nurses sent to France in 1917. In the following remembrance, she comments on her state during the last months of the war.

DURING THE LONG HOURS, we couldn't stop to eat. Just grab a bite off the mess cart, or a cup of coffee. It was awful to see those poor kids [the soldiers] strapped on a board with their backs broken, or an arm or both legs off. It was terribly trying on our nerves.

I got so nervous, I couldn't relax when it was over. I couldn't sleep. They found me walking in the street wearing just my pajamas, saying I had to get back on duty. . . . That's when I wound up in the hospital myself. They gave me warm baths and some sedatives. About then, my father hadn't heard from me in a long time, so he wrote to Washington. They wrote back that I was in the hospital suffering from "shell shock."

—*From Lettie Gavin,* American Women in World War I: They Also Served. *Niwot, CO: University Press of Colorado, 1997.*

THINK ABOUT THIS

1. Why did the writer have a difficult time getting over her experience?

2. What is shell shock?

"Can Vegetables Fruit and the Kaiser too": This poster used humor to encourage Americans on the home front to do their part by conserving food.

Chapter 7

The Home Front

AMERICANS GEARED UP to fight the war with every-thing they had. The government sounded the clarion call. The Food Administration urged housewives to substitute other foods for meat and wheat on specific days of the week. The National War Garden Commission asked families to plant gardens and to can fruits and vegetables from their household plots. "Can Vegetables, Fruit, and the Kaiser, too" proclaimed a poster for the commission. Children were told to save quarters and use them to buy war savings stamps ("Lick a stamp and lick the Kaiser") and to save ordinary household goods such as old glass and empty cans for reuse by war factories. Schools taught lessons around the themes of patriotism, service, and self-sacrifice. "Every patriotic American can serve by being loyal—by working, saving, giving" proclaimed *Our Country's Call to Service: A Manual of Patriotic Activities Through the Schools,* published in 1918. The Treasury Department staged huge rallies during which all Americans were asked to buy Liberty bonds to fund the war. The War Industries Board persuaded factories to increase their production of war goods.

During this time, a new kind of worker appeared in the U.S. workplace. American women welcomed the chance to enter the workforce and willingly took over as mechanics, welders, machinists, postal workers, elevator operators—jobs once held only by men. They toiled long hours to help the war effort and managed to work at home, too. The war also witnessed the mass movement of people from one part of the nation to another. Shortages of workers in the factories of the North and Midwest created opportunities for hundreds of thousands of African Americans from the South. During the war years, migrants from the heavily agricultural South

As their counterparts overseas had done several years before, thousands of American women went to work once the United States entered the war. This photograph, hand-colored with oil paints, shows women welders working in a munitions factory.

traveled north, where they established black neighborhoods in cities such as Chicago, Detroit, and New York. The war was changing America in important ways.

Women at Work: A Magazine Article

World War I was the first time in U.S. history that women in large numbers took jobs traditionally held by men. They became conductors on streetcars, automobile mechanics, and shipyard workers. Many worked on the assembly lines of factories making tanks, trucks, and munitions. For the most part, women liked the challenge of their new lives. The attitude of these women is described in the following excerpt from an interview by Norma Kastl, an interviewer in a service bureau for women workers. Her interview appeared in a magazine published during the war.

THE GOVERNMENT GAS MASK factory has proved a most interesting field for many artists, musicians, and stage women. One well-known portrait painter is now spending her days in turning over little brass disks and carefully inspecting both sides. Another woman who has created several famous character parts on Broadway gets up every morning at half past five and takes the early train into New York to get to the factory at eight o'clock. During the recent speeding-up period, caused by urgent calls from our armies overseas, she reached home often as late as ten or eleven at night. But did she mind? Not she! "I

"It has been one of the richest experiences of my life . . . feeling that I was being really useful to the boys on the other side."

would not have missed it for anything," she said. "It has been one of the richest experiences of my life—meeting all the wonderful women who are there . . . and all the time feeling that I was being really useful to the boys on the other side."

—From Norma B. Kastl, "Wartime, the Place and the Girl," Independent *magazine, date unknown.*

THINK ABOUT THIS

1. How do you think the writer used irony to compare the level of work the women had been doing with the jobs they were now performing in the gas mask factory?
2. Why were the women so satisfied with their new work?

Raising Money for the War: The Liberty Loan Drive

The United States was committed to victory, but the cost of supporting an army overseas was huge. The government asked the American people to help finance the war effort and held four campaigns to sell Liberty bonds. Everyone was asked to buy bonds. Celebrities—from opera singers to movie stars—encouraged Americans to do their bit by buying bonds. In the end, the United States made more than $20 billion for the war. The Special Assistant Secretary of War launched the Fourth Liberty Loan Campaign among African Americans in the District of Columbia in October 1918. Here is part of his speech.

"Let us buy bonds—and then buy more bonds!"

THIS IS AS THE PRESIDENT [Woodrow Wilson] says, the people's war. It is not a white man's war. It is not a black man's war. It is a war of all the people under the Stars and Stripes for the preservation of human liberty throughout the world.

Already, the Negro has responded promptly and cheerfully to the call for his *man-power,* and three times since the declaration of war against the Imperial German Government he has answered generously, readily, and without stint to the call for his *money-power.*

Now comes a fourth call for financial aid. . . .

Appropriately—in view of the onward march of General Pershing's

One of the famous World War I posters asked U.S. citizens to help support the war—and keep Germans off American soil. The black eagle crest on the boots was a symbol of the German Empire.

Invincible Crusaders on France's western front, the Fourth Liberty Loan is styled "The Fighting Loan." Black men are among these Crusaders. We who must remain at home are in duty bound to lend the limit of our aid to those who have gone abroad. . . . We cannot do this in a more effective way than to offer our dollars to sustain the Government . . . and its fighting men while they are braving death, to insure freedom and justice to all mankind.

The success of the Fourth Liberty Loan should overtop all of its predecessors in the volume of subscriptions . . . and this should be the absorbing mission of colored ministers, editors, teachers, merchants, lawyers, doctors, and speakers and workers day by day and night by night until that objective is gained. "He gives twice who gives quickly." Let us buy bonds—and then buy more bonds!

—*From Emmett J. Scott,* Scott's Official History of the American Negro in the World War. *New York: Arno Press and the* New York Times, *1969.*

THINK ABOUT THIS

1. In light of the prejudice African Americans had long endured, does this speech ring true?
2. To whom did the speaker compare the black soldier? How does this comparison appeal to black pride?

On the Lookout for Spies: The Committee on Public Information Issues a Warning

The Committee on Public Information was set up in 1917 to whip up patriotism and support for the war. Its director was newspaperman George Creel. The committee hired men and women to deliver brief but stirring patriotic speeches (on themes such as "Save Food," "Buy Bonds," and "Give Until It Hurts") in places such as movie theaters and concert halls. Boy Scouts were given the job of handing out patriotic pamphlets. Famous artists and writers were hired to draw patriotic posters and write advertisements in support of the war. Citizens were also warned to be on the lookout for spies. Here is an excerpt from the Committee's warning:

GERMAN AGENTS ARE EVERYWHERE, eager to gather scraps of news about our men, our ships, our munitions. It is still possible to get such information through to Germany, where thousands of these fragments . . . are pieced together into a whole which spells death to American soldiers and danger to American homes.

- DO NOT discuss in public, or with strangers, any news of troop and transport movements, or bits of gossip as to our military preparations, which come into your possession.

- DO NOT permit your friends in service to tell you—or write you—"inside" facts about where they are, what they are doing and seeing.

"German agents are everywhere."

- DO NOT become a tool of the Hun by passing on the malicious, disheartening rumors which he so eagerly sows.

- AND DO NOT wait until you catch someone putting a bomb under a factory. Report the man who spreads pessimistic stories, divulges—or seeks—confidential military information, cries for peace, or belittles our efforts to win the war.

Send the names of such persons, even if they are in uniform, to the Department of Justice, Washington. Give all the details you can, with names of witnesses if possible. . . .

COMMITTEE ON PUBLIC INFORMATION
8 JACKSON PLACE
WASHINGTON, D.C.

—*From Committee on Public Information poster, date unknown.*

THINK ABOUT THIS

1. According to this warning, what were some of the dangers facing the United States during the war?
2. How do you think this document affected German Americans?
3. How do you think this document affected Americans' constitutional liberties?

Chapter 8

War As Seen By . . .

WAR IS A MONUMENTAL, terrible event. Few can remain untouched by its horrors. World War I saw an outpouring of classic writings from those who experienced it. Novels such as Erich Maria Remarque's *All Quiet on the Western Front* and Ernest Hemingway's *A Farewell to Arms* still illuminate war's effect on its participants. Poets such as Alan Seeger, Wilfred Owen, and John McCrae expressed eternal truths about war in their poetry. Some of the most vivid writing about World War I is by the correspondents who witnessed the battles firsthand and lived with the ordinary soldiers.

Newspapers and press associations sent out scores of writers to cover the action despite the military's attempt to censor, or limit, their reporting. Some of the most famous correspondents of the war were Will Irwin, Ring Lardner, Floyd Gibbons, Edwin L. James, John T. McCutcheon, Frazier Hunt, and Westbrook Pegler, who at twenty-three was the youngest correspondent. Women reported from the front, too. Peggy Hull Deuell visited troop camps and spent several months with an infantry brigade.

All Quiet on the Western Front, the famous novel by Erich Maria Remarque, is told from the perspective of a young German soldier. Remarque himself had been drafted into the German army at age eighteen and was wounded several times. The vivid accounts of poets and writers like Remarque, who lived through the war, provide us with remarkable portrayals of an extraordinary time.

Richard Harding Davis was probably the most famous correspondent of the war. His reports from the front kept Americans informed of what was happening on the battlefields. Davis expressed his belief in the importance of the correspondent's job when he stated, "This is a world war, and the world has the right to know, not what is going to happen next, but at least what has happened. If men died nobly, if women and children have suffered, if cities have been wrecked, the world should know that. Some men are trained to fight, and others are trained to write. The latter can tell you of what they have seen so that you can also see it." You'll read some of Davis's words and those of other eyewitnesses in this chapter.

A Newspaperman Describes the Dead

Richard Harding Davis made the war real for hundreds of Americans. Here is part of his description of the aftermath of a battle.

AFTER THE GERMANS WERE repulsed at Meaux and at Sezanne the dead of both armies were so many that they lay intermingled in layers three and four deep. They were buried in long pits and piled on top of each other like cigars in a box. Lines of fresh earth so long that you mistook them for trenches intended to conceal regiments, were in reality graves. Some bodies lay for days uncovered until they lost all human semblance. They were so many you ceased to regard them even as corpses. They had become just part of the waste, a part of the shattered walls, uprooted trees,

> "What once had been your fellow men were only bundles of clothes, swollen and shapeless, like scarecrows stuffed with rags."

and fields ploughed by shells. What once had been your fellow men were only bundles of clothes, swollen and shapeless, like scarecrows stuffed with rags, polluting the air.

—From Richard Harding Davis, as quoted in Hooray for Peace, Hurrah for War by Steven Jantzen. New York: Alfred A. Knopf, 1971.

THINK ABOUT THIS

1. What tone did Davis set in this selection?
2. How might the military react to Davis's account?
3. What would you have thought of war if you had read this during World War I?

A Soldier and Poet Writes from a Trench in France

Alan Seeger was an American poet who served in the French Foreign Legion during World War I. Seeger was born in New York City in 1888. He studied literature at Harvard and contributed his poetry to the *Harvard Monthly*. After graduation, Seeger moved to Paris, France, where he planned to continue his writing. When war broke out in 1914, Seeger decided that he had to fight for freedom and for France, his adopted home.

While serving in the Legion, Seeger found time to write numerous letters and poems. His most famous poem is "I Have a Rendezvous with Death."

This is what Alan Seeger had to say about his experiences in the trenches. His observations appeared in letters to the *New York Sun* in the first years of the war. Seeger died on July 4, 1916, while charging a German machine-gun nest. He was twenty-eight years old.

THIS STYLE OF WARFARE IS extremely modern and for the artillerymen is doubtless very interesting, but for the poor common soldier it is anything but romantic. His role is simply to dig himself a hole in the ground and to keep hidden in it as tightly as possible. Continually under the fire of the opposing batteries, he is yet never allowed to get a glimpse of the enemy. Exposed to the dangers of war . . . he is condemned to sit like an animal in its burrow and hear the shells whistle over his head and take their little daily toll from his comrades. . . .

His feet are numb, his canteen frozen, but he is not allowed . . . to light a candle, but must fold himself in his blanket and lie down cramped in the dirty straw to sleep as best he may.

Cramped quarters breed ill temper and disputes. The impossibility of the simplest kind of personal cleanliness make vermin a universal ill against which there is no remedy. . . .

Six days is the regular period for service in the trenches under normal conditions. Often enough it seems close to the limit of physical and moral strain which a man can bear. The last night the company packs up its belongings and either in the twilight of the evening or dawn assembles and waits for the shadowy arrival of the relieving sections to whom the position is surrendered without regret.

—*From Alan Seeger, in a letter to the* New York Sun, *December 8, 1914.*

THINK ABOUT THIS

1. How long was the period of service for soldiers in the trenches?
2. What do you think Seeger meant when he called the warfare "modern"?
3. Why, in Seeger's opinion, is fighting an "invisible" enemy so demoralizing?

"You Get Scared": A Wartime Remembrance by Herman Warner

Dr. Herman Warner was born in 1897 on the island of Jamaica. He served in the British West Indies Forces from the middle of 1916 to 1918. He saw action on the Western Front, in Belgium, where some of the fiercest fighting took place. When the war ended, Warner came to the United States and settled in Harlem in New York City. He graduated from Howard University Medical School and practiced medicine in Harlem. Dr. Warner died in 1988. In this recollection, Herman Warner recounts his war years.

I SAW HAND-TO-HAND COMBAT. You get scared. Anybody who tells you that he was not scared is a liar. There is a line of demarcation between fear and cowardice. When your buddy falls next to you, you regret it, but you're glad it wasn't you. You mourn for the person, but the French have an expression, *sauve qui peut*—"save yourself if you can."

I thought about the idea of killing another man. I came from a religious background, and at times you would feel, "What am I doing here?" Just the thought of killing a person. But then you get completely conditioned, not only to the environment but to that way of life. So many years, you were taken up with escape, just trying to get away, that you didn't have enough time to look at the individuals you were fighting. And you didn't always kill. Sometimes you would maim, and then go on about your business, depending on your situation. It's horrible, but it then shows you how complex a human being is. You know, I'm the most peaceful man in the world.

—*From Jeff Kisseloff,* You Must Remember This: An Oral History of Manhattan from the 1890s to World War II. *New York: Schocken Books, 1989.*

1. What do you think Dr. Warner meant by the statement, "There is a line of demarcation between fear and cowardice"?

2. How does he explain the apparent contradiction between being a peace-loving, gentle person and being a soldier?

"The Cathedral of Rheims": A Poem by Joyce Kilmer

Joyce Kilmer was born in New Brunswick, New Jersey, in 1886. He studied at Rutgers College and Columbia University. After graduation, Kilmer worked as a newspaperman for the *New York Times*. His poem "Trees" appeared in *Poetry* magazine in 1913 and won Kilmer national fame. Joyce Kilmer served in France and was killed in 1918 while attacking a German machine-gun nest.

The following excerpt is from the poem "The Cathedral of Rheims," in which Kilmer describes the medieval cathedral of Rheims, France.

He who walks through the meadows of Champagne
    At noon in Fall, when leaves like gold appear,
     Sees it draw near
Like some great mountain set upon the plain,
From radiant dawn until the close of day,
     Nearer it grows
     To him who goes
Across the country. When tall towers lay
Their shadowy pall
     Upon his way,
     He enters, where

The solid stone is hollowed deep by all
Its centuries of beauty and prayer. . . .

Sacred through art, from pinnacle to base:
And in thy panes of gold and scarlet glass
The setting sun sees thousandfold his face;
Sorrow and joy, in stately silence pass
Across thy walls, the shadow and the light;
Around thy lofty pillars, tapers white
Illuminate, with delicate sharp flames
The brows of saints with venerable names,
And in the night erect a fiery wall.
A great but silent fervour burns in all
Those simple folk who kneel, pathetic, dumb,
And know that down below, beside the Rhine—
Cannon, horses, soldiers, flags in line—
With blare of trumpets, mighty armies come.

Now war has come, and peace is at an end.

—From Joyce Kilmer, Poems, Essays and Letters. *New York:*
George H. Doran Publishers, 1918.

THINK ABOUT THIS

1. To what does the poet compare the cathedral?
2. While people are praying inside, what is taking place outside the cathedral walls?
3. What comment do you think Kilmer was making about ordinary people caught up in war?
4. Why do you think Kilmer chose to write a war poem about a cathedral?

The Most Famous Poem of World War I: "In Flanders Fields"

John McCrae (1872–1918), a Canadian soldier, doctor, and poet, composed the most well-known poem of World War I. McCrae wrote "In Flanders Fields" the day after one of his closest friends was killed in battle. (Flanders is the region in western Belgium bordering on France where much fighting took place.) The simple wooden cross that marked his friend's grave inspired McCrae to write the following lines. The poppy, a bright red flower, became the symbol of the war and is still used to recall the dead on days of remembrance.

"We shall not sleep, though poppies grow in Flanders fields."

In Flanders fields the poppies blow
Between the crosses, row on row
That mark our place; and in the sky
The larks still bravely singing, fly
Scarce heard amid the guns below.

We are the Dead. Short days ago
We lived, felt dawn, saw sunset glow.
Loved, and were loved, and now we lie
In Flanders fields.

Take up our quarrel with the foe;
To you from failing hands we throw
The torch, be yours to hold it high.

If ye break faith with us who die
We shall not sleep, though poppies grow
In Flanders fields.

—John McCrae, "In Flanders Fields," 1919.

THINK ABOUT THIS

1. Who is the speaker in this poem?

2. What does he want?

3. What will happen if faith is broken with the dead?

"Armistice Signed, End of the War!" A *New York Times* headline heralds what Americans prayed would mark the end of troubled times.

Chapter 9

The End

PEACE CAME IN NOVEMBER 1918 with the surrender of Germany. Its army could not hold out against the Allies once American troops were in the fight. American soldiers were not the only factor that brought the war to a close. Food from American farms and money from U.S. Treasury loans helped win the war for the Allies.

Unlike its partners, the United States did not want to punish defeated Germany. Even before the fighting stopped, President Wilson called for a plan that would address the problems that had led to war in the first place. His high-minded goal was to prevent future wars. He took part in the Versailles peace conference and while there insisted that the delegates establish the Covenant, the constitution of the League of Nations. Yet Wilson could do nothing to stop the Allies from imposing harsh penalties on Germany and the Central Powers. The other Allies disregarded the principle of self-determination, one of the Fourteen Points Wilson had outlined to Congress the year before as necessary steps for peace. The Allies took over German territories in Africa and the Pacific as mandates—lands under their control through the supervision of the League of Nations. Wilson did not help his cause. His explanation of the League of Nations did not convince Congress to support it, and most Americans did not understand why the nation should join this organization. When the time came for the Senate to ratify the peace treaty, it refused to do so. The United States rejected the Treaty of Versailles, and it never joined the League of Nations.

In just nine short years, the nation would fall into a terrible economic depression—and ultimately another world war. In the post–World War I period, the former Allies showed no will to correct the ills that led to the Great War or to anticipate and deal with aggressive actions by Germany, Japan, and Italy. Across the Atlantic, Americans could little understand the deeply felt national hatreds that would produce World War II.

A Plan for Peace: Woodrow Wilson's Fourteen Points

President Wilson outlined his plan for peace in a speech he delivered to a joint session of Congress on January 8, 1918. This came after the Allies failed to agree on their aims in the war. Wilson's plan was accepted by the Allies but only reluctantly. Here are some of the points from the president's plan.

WHAT WE DEMAND in this war . . . is that the world be made fit and safe to live in; and particularly that it be made safe for every peace-loving nation. . . . The program of the world's peace, therefore, is our program; and that program . . . as we see it, is this:

I. Open covenants of peace, openly arrived at, after which there shall be no private international understandings of any kind but diplomacy shall proceed always frankly and in the public view.

II. Absolute freedom of navigation upon the seas, outside territorial waters, alike in peace and in war. . . .

III. The removal, so far as possible, of all economic barriers and the establishment of an equality of trade conditions among all the nations consenting to the peace. . . .

IV. Adequate guarantees given and taken that national armaments will be reduced to the lowest point consistent with domestic safety.

V. A free, open-minded, and absolutely impartial adjustment of all colonial claims. . . .

VI. The evacuation of all Russian territory and such settlement of all questions affecting Russia as will secure . . . for her . . . an opportunity for the independent determination of her own political development. . . .

VII. Belgium . . . must be evacuated and restored. . . .

VIII. All French territory should be freed and the invaded portions restored. . . .

IX. A readjustment of the frontiers of Italy . . . along clearly recognizable lines of nationality.

X. The peoples of Austria-Hungary . . . should be accorded the freest opportunity of autonomous development.

XI. Rumania, Serbia, and Montenegro should be evacuated; occupied territories restored; Serbia accorded free and secure access to the sea; and the relations of the several Balkan states to one another determined by friendly counsel along historically established lines of allegiance and nationality. . . .

XII. The Turkish portions of the present Ottoman Empire should be assured a secure sovereignty . . . and the Dardanelles should be permanently opened as a free passage to the ships and commerce of all nations under international guarantees.

American soldiers are shown celebrating the armistice in this hand-painted photograph from November 11, 1918.

XIII. An independent Polish state should be erected....

XIV. A general association of nations must be formed ... for the purpose of affording mutual guarantees of political independence and territorial integrity to great and small states alike.

We have no jealousy of German greatness.... We do not wish to injure her or to block in any way her legitimate influence of power. We do not wish to fight her either with arms or with hostile arrangements of trade if she is willing to associate herself with us and the other peace-loving nations of the world in covenants of justice and law and fair dealing.

—From Congressional Record: *Vol. LVI, 1918, pt. I: pp. 680–681.*

1. What are some of the key words Wilson used in this document?
2. What did Wilson hope to achieve in point fourteen?
3. How do you think a Pole would have reacted to Wilson's Fourteen Points? A German?

The Armistice Is Signed: How the War Came to an End

World War I officially ended on the eleventh hour of the eleventh day of the eleventh month of 1918. The following is a description of how the news came to the world.

THE WAR CAME TO AN END on Monday, Nov. 11, 1918 at 11 o'clock A.M., French time; 6 o'clock Washington time. The armistice, which was imposed upon Germany by the Allies and the United States, was signed by the German plenipotentiaries at 5 o'clock A.M., Paris time; midnight, Washington time.

The conclusion of the armistice followed within three weeks after the dispatch of a note from the German Government to President Wilson, in which it was affirmed that a fundamental change had been made in the German Government and asking that steps be taken to arrange an armistice.

"The war came to an end on Monday, Nov. 11, 1918 at 11 o'clock A.M."

On Oct. 23 President Wilson replied by agreeing to take up with the Allies the question of an armistice. On Oct. 25 a dispatch was allowed to go from Berlin [the capital of Germany] stating that an enormous crowd had assembled before the Reichstag building calling for the abdication of the Kaiser and the formation of a republic.

On Oct. 31 the representatives of the allied Governments held a formal meeting at Versailles [a town outside of Paris] to consider the armistice terms for Austria, which would foreshadow the terms to be submitted to Germany. . . .

The Supreme War Council resumed its sessions at Versailles on Nov. 1 to consider the armistice terms which would be submitted to Austria and Germany. . . .

On Nov. 3 the armistice with Austria was signed in the field. On Nov. 6, it was announced from Berlin that a German delegation to conclude an armistice and take up peace negotiations had left for the western front. . . .

The [German] delegates crossed the allied line near La Capelle late on the night of Nov. 7. The white-flag bearers . . . arrived . . . within the French lines about 2 o'clock A.M., Nov. 8, and passed the remainder of the night there. They were taken to a house at Rethondes, six miles east of Compiegne and thirty miles from Marshal Foch's [the head of French forces] headquarters, where preparations had been made to receive them.

The automobiles conveying the delegates carried white flags and were preceded by a trumpeter. Some French soldiers under an officer approached them on the road just outside the lines.

The delegates established their identity and showed their credentials. The members of the German party were then blindfolded and the delegates proceeded to the place where they spent the night.

The delegates were received by Marshal Foch at Rethondes at 9 o'clock on the morning of Nov. 8, in a railroad car, in which the Commander in Chief of the allied force had his headquarters.

Marshal Foch then read the terms in a loud voice, dwelling upon each word. The Germans were prepared by semi-official communications for the stipulations as a whole, but hearing set forth in detail the concrete demands seemed to bring to them for the first time full realization of the extent of the German defeat.

The abdication of the Kaiser and the revolution in Germany occurred the day following the receipt of the armistice terms, Nov. 9, but no decision was announced respecting the acceptance of the armistice.

The German courier bearing the text of the armistice conditions arrived at German headquarters at 10 o'clock A.M., Nov. 10. The courier, Captain Helldorf, was long delayed while the German batteries persisted in bombarding the route he had to follow.

Nineteen hours after the German courier reached the German headquarters—at 5 o'clock A.M. Paris time, Nov. 11—the armistice was signed and the official announcement was made at Washington at 2:40 A.M., Nov. 11, by the Secretary of State. President Wilson was notified immediately by telephone.

—From staff article in New York Times Current History, *December 1918.*

Think about This

1. Who imposed the armistice on whom?
2. When was the armistice signed?
3. Why do you think the Allies took such pains to state the terms of the armistice?

The Last Shots of the War Are Fired: A Firsthand Account

News of the signing of the armistice spread across the Western Front. Soldiers on both sides of the conflict knew this was the end of four long years of fighting. Here is how one American soldier, Lieutenant Walter Davenport, described what happened in the area around St. Mihiel, France.

ABOUT 9:30 A.M. ON NOVEMBER 11TH, the Germans must have gotten word that the Armistice had been signed. We were dug in the mud of the Bois de Dommartin. . . . Every Boche gun between Dommartin and Metz opened up on us. My God, how they strafed us. Everything from minenwerfers to 210's [kinds of German artillery] descended upon those woods. The soft ground billowed like the ocean. But . . . our casualties were very, very small. And our artillery came back at them. From 10 o'clock to 11—the hour for the cessation of hostilities—the opposing batteries simply raised hell. It was not a barrage. It was a deluge.

> *"It was 10:60 precisely and—the roar stopped like a motor car hitting a wall."*

All along our front the earth was flying skyward geyser-like. And above us roared about 50 Allied planes watching the effect of our shots. . . . I do not know how many thousand tons of steel, copper . . . and lead were poured into, over, and upon Jerry, but it was fearful to see.

It was 10:60 precisely and—the roar stopped like a motor car hitting a wall. The resulting quiet was uncanny in comparison. From somewhere far below ground, Germans began to appear. They clambered to the parapets and began to shout wildly. They threw their rifles, hats, bandoleers, bayonets and trench knives toward us. They began to sing.

—From Frank Freidel, Over There: The Story of America's First Great Overseas Crusade. *Boston: Little, Brown and Company, 1964.*

THINK ABOUT THIS

1. What images does the writer use to describe the last shots fired?
2. What did the German soldiers do at the end of the barrage? Why do you think they did this?

This message, which was received on the front line, announced to American troops that the war was over: "Hostilities will cease at 1100 on Nov 11."

Sleeping Forever: A Writer Memorializes the Unknown Soldier

In 1921 the United States was in the midst of a period of fun, free-spending, and fortune-building. This time in the nation's history came to be known as the Jazz Age or the Roaring Twenties. The war and its miseries were gone but not erased from memory. In November 1921, the remains of an unidentified American soldier were brought from a grave in France for a military funeral and burial in Arlington National Cemetery in Washington, D.C. Kirke L. Simpson, a member of the Associated Press, a wire service, wrote about the event over three days—November 9, 10, and 11. Simpson was awarded the 1922 Pulitzer Prize in Reporting for these pieces. The following is an excerpt from the third and final article.

"Out there in the broad avenue was a simple soldier, dead for honor of the flag. He was nameless."

UNDER THE WIDE AND STARRY skies of his own homeland America's unknown dead from France sleeps tonight, a soldier home from the wars....

All day long the nation poured out its heart in pride and glory for the nameless American. Before the first crash of the minute guns roared its knell for the dead from the shadow of the Washington Monument, the people who claim him as their own were trooping out to do him honor. They lined the long road from the Capitol to the hillside where he sleeps tonight . . . they choked the bridges that lead across the river to the fields of the brave, in which he is the last comer.

As he was carried past through the banks of humanity that lined Pennsylvania Avenue a solemn, reverant hush held the living walls....

Out there in the broad avenue was a simple soldier, dead for honor of the flag. He was nameless. No man knew what part in the great life of the nation he had filled when last he passed over his home soil. But in France he had died as Americans always have been ready to die, for the flag and what it means....

Lifted by his hero-bearers from the stage, the unknown was carried in his flag-wrapped, simple coffin out the wide sweep of the terrace. The bearers laid the sleeper down above the crypt, on which had been placed a little of the soil of France....

A rocking blast of gunfire rang from the woods. The glittering circle of bayonets stiffened to a salute to the dead....

High and clear and true . . . a bugle lifted the old, old notes of taps....

Fades the light;
And afar
Goeth day, cometh night,
And a star,
Leadeth all, speedeth all,
To their rest.

The guns roared out again in the national salute. He was home, The Unknown, to sleep forever among his own.

—*From Kirke L. Simpson, "America's Unknown Dead from France Sleeps Tonight," 1921.*

THINK ABOUT THIS

1. How did the American people react to the burying of the soldier?

2. Why does the nation honor a soldier whose name nobody knows?

Turning Our Backs: Woodrow Wilson's Radio Address, 1923

For Wilson, the end of the war brought only personal defeat. He suffered a devastating stroke that left him in ill health. Americans rejected the Covenant, the League of Nations' constitution. And Congress never ratified the Treaty of Versailles, which Wilson had helped to draft. Wilson did not run in the presidential election of 1920, but the candidate from his political party, the Democratic Party, pledged to take the United States into the League. The election outcome proved that Americans wanted to forget the war. Voters chose Republican Warren G. Harding, who promised "a return to normalcy," as their new president.

"When the victory was won . . . we turned our backs upon our associates . . . and withdrew into a sullen and selfish isolation."

Three years later, on November 10, 1923, former president Woodrow Wilson gave a speech on the radio in honor of Armistice Day, the anniversary of the war's end. He reminded Americans of what they had won in the Great War, urging listeners to continue taking part in the affairs of the world—for the peace and democracy American soldiers had died to preserve. The following is an excerpt from that speech.

THE ANNIVERSARY OF ARMISTICE DAY should stir us to great exaltation of spirit because of the proud recollection that it was our day . . . which lifted the world to the high levels of vision and achievement upon which the great war for democracy and right was fought and won. . . . When the victory was won . . . we turned our backs upon our associates [the Allies] and refused to bear any responsible part in the administration of peace . . . and withdrew into a sullen and selfish isolation. . . .

That we should have thus done a great wrong to civilization at one of the most critical turning points in the history of the world is the more to be deplored because every anxious year that has followed has made the need for such services as we might have rendered more and more evident and more and more pressing. . . .

The affairs of the world can be set straight only by the firmest and most determined exhibition of the will to lead and make the right prevail.

—From Woodrow Wilson's radio address, November 10, 1923.

THINK ABOUT THIS

1. Why did Wilson disapprove of America's actions after World War I?

2. What do you think he meant by the "will to lead"?

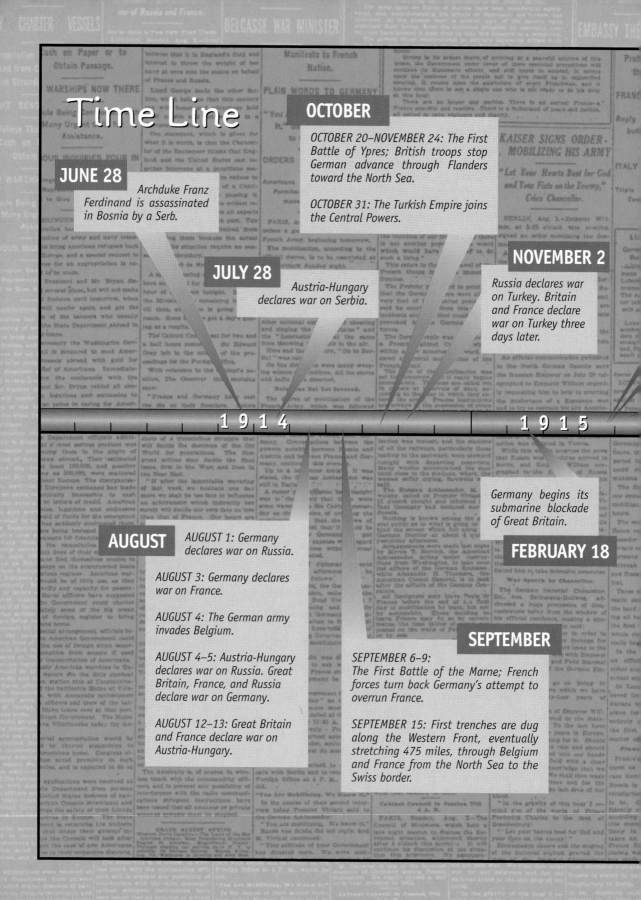

Time Line

JUNE 28

Archduke Franz Ferdinand is assassinated in Bosnia by a Serb.

JULY 28

Austria-Hungary declares war on Serbia.

OCTOBER

OCTOBER 20–NOVEMBER 24: The First Battle of Ypres; British troops stop German advance through Flanders toward the North Sea.

OCTOBER 31: The Turkish Empire joins the Central Powers.

NOVEMBER 2

Russia declares war on Turkey. Britain and France declare war on Turkey three days later.

1 9 1 4

1 9 1 5

AUGUST

AUGUST 1: Germany declares war on Russia.

AUGUST 3: Germany declares war on France.

AUGUST 4: The German army invades Belgium.

AUGUST 4–5: Austria-Hungary declares war on Russia. Great Britain, France, and Russia declare war on Germany.

AUGUST 12–13: Great Britain and France declare war on Austria-Hungary.

SEPTEMBER

SEPTEMBER 6–9: The First Battle of the Marne; French forces turn back Germany's attempt to overrun France.

SEPTEMBER 15: First trenches are dug along the Western Front, eventually stretching 475 miles, through Belgium and France from the North Sea to the Swiss border.

FEBRUARY 18

Germany begins its submarine blockade of Great Britain.

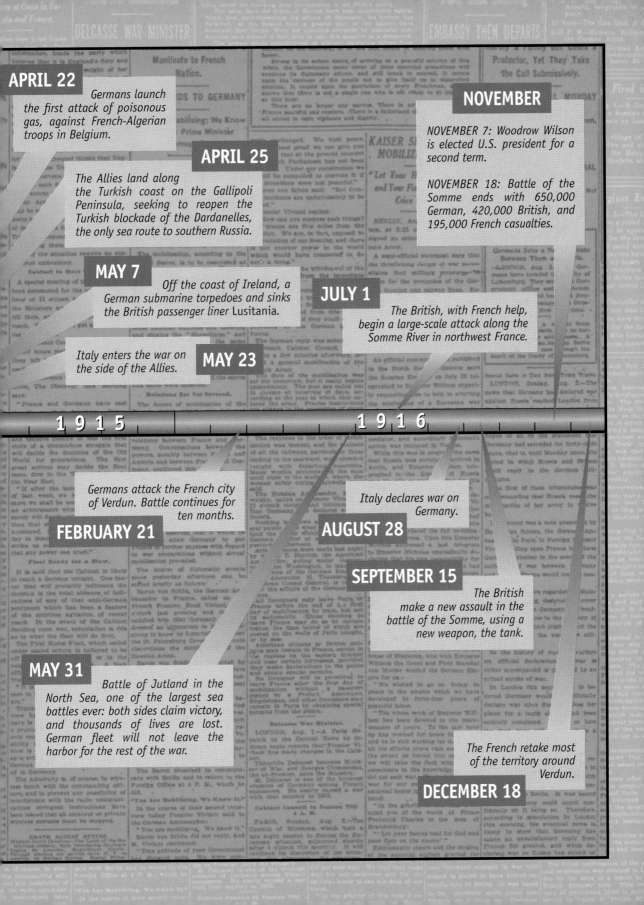

APRIL 22

Germans launch the first attack of poisonous gas, against French-Algerian troops in Belgium.

APRIL 25

The Allies land along the Turkish coast on the Gallipoli Peninsula, seeking to reopen the Turkish blockade of the Dardanelles, the only sea route to southern Russia.

MAY 7

Off the coast of Ireland, a German submarine torpedoes and sinks the British passenger liner Lusitania.

Italy enters the war on the side of the Allies. **MAY 23**

NOVEMBER

NOVEMBER 7: Woodrow Wilson is elected U.S. president for a second term.

NOVEMBER 18: Battle of the Somme ends with 650,000 German, 420,000 British, and 195,000 French casualties.

JULY 1

The British, with French help, begin a large-scale attack along the Somme River in northwest France.

1 9 1 5   **1 9 1 6**

Germans attack the French city of Verdun. Battle continues for ten months.

FEBRUARY 21

Italy declares war on Germany.

AUGUST 28

SEPTEMBER 15

The British make a new assault in the battle of the Somme, using a new weapon, the tank.

MAY 31

Battle of Jutland in the North Sea, one of the largest sea battles ever: both sides claim victory, and thousands of lives are lost. German fleet will not leave the harbor for the rest of the war.

The French retake most of the territory around Verdun.

DECEMBER 18

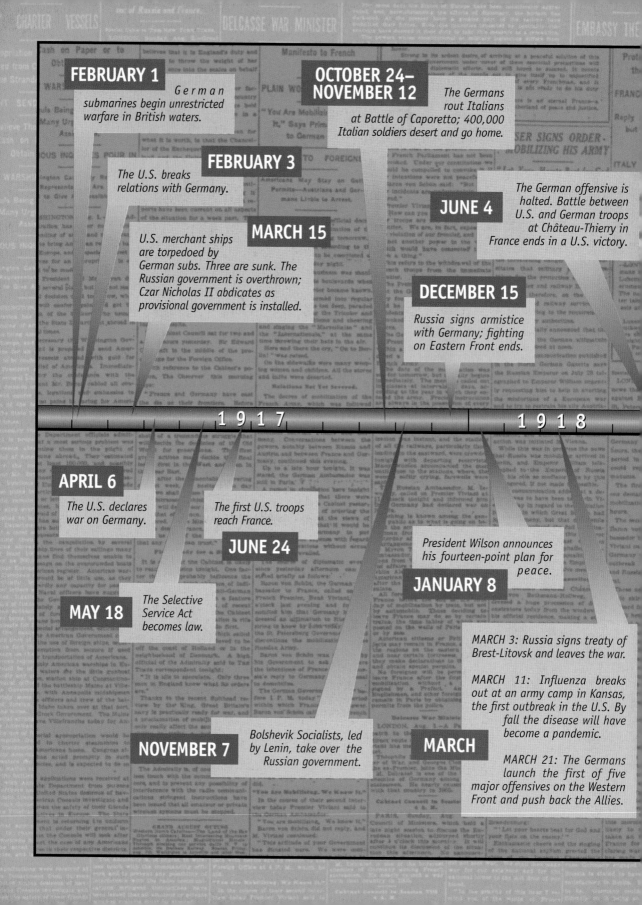

FEBRUARY 1

German submarines begin unrestricted warfare in British waters.

OCTOBER 24–NOVEMBER 12

The Germans rout Italians at Battle of Caporetto; 400,000 Italian soldiers desert and go home.

FEBRUARY 3

The U.S. breaks relations with Germany.

MARCH 15

U.S. merchant ships are torpedoed by German subs. Three are sunk. The Russian government is overthrown; Czar Nicholas II abdicates as provisional government is installed.

JUNE 4

The German offensive is halted. Battle between U.S. and German troops at Château-Thierry in France ends in a U.S. victory.

DECEMBER 15

Russia signs armistice with Germany; fighting on Eastern Front ends.

1 9 1 7

1 9 1 8

APRIL 6

The U.S. declares war on Germany.

The first U.S. troops reach France.

JUNE 24

President Wilson announces his fourteen-point plan for peace.

JANUARY 8

MAY 18

The Selective Service Act becomes law.

MARCH 3: Russia signs treaty of Brest-Litovsk and leaves the war.

MARCH 11: Influenza breaks out at an army camp in Kansas, the first outbreak in the U.S. By fall the disease will have become a pandemic.

NOVEMBER 7

Bolshevik Socialists, led by Lenin, take over the Russian government.

MARCH

MARCH 21: The Germans launch the first of five major offensives on the Western Front and push back the Allies.

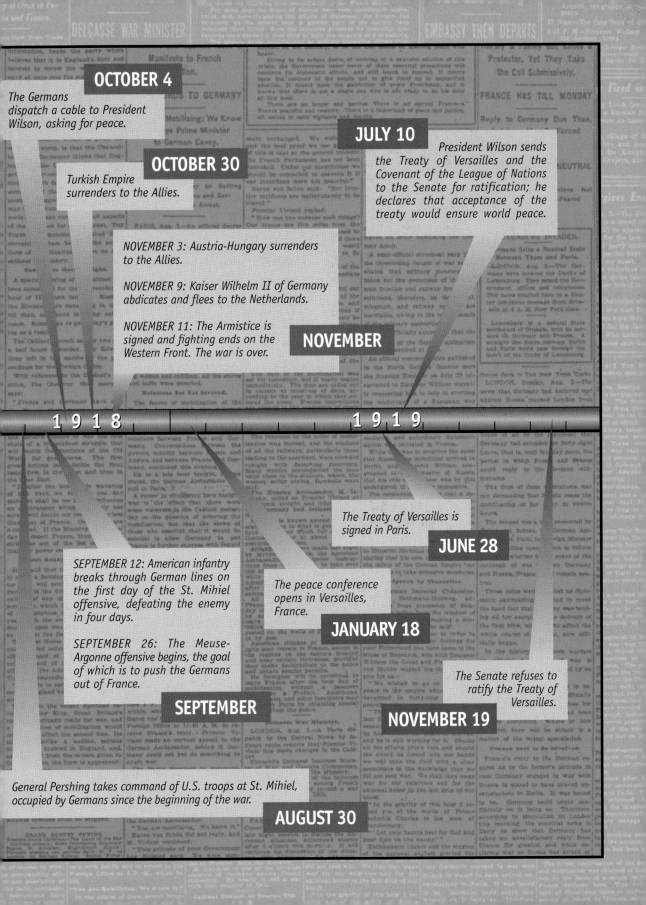

OCTOBER 4

The Germans dispatch a cable to President Wilson, asking for peace.

OCTOBER 30

Turkish Empire surrenders to the Allies.

JULY 10

President Wilson sends the Treaty of Versailles and the Covenant of the League of Nations to the Senate for ratification; he declares that acceptance of the treaty would ensure world peace.

NOVEMBER 3: Austria-Hungary surrenders to the Allies.

NOVEMBER 9: Kaiser Wilhelm II of Germany abdicates and flees to the Netherlands.

NOVEMBER 11: The Armistice is signed and fighting ends on the Western Front. The war is over.

NOVEMBER

1 9 1 8

1 9 1 9

The Treaty of Versailles is signed in Paris.

JUNE 28

SEPTEMBER 12: American infantry breaks through German lines on the first day of the St. Mihiel offensive, defeating the enemy in four days.

SEPTEMBER 26: The Meuse-Argonne offensive begins, the goal of which is to push the Germans out of France.

The peace conference opens in Versailles, France.

JANUARY 18

SEPTEMBER

The Senate refuses to ratify the Treaty of Versailles.

NOVEMBER 19

General Pershing takes command of U.S. troops at St. Mihiel, occupied by Germans since the beginning of the war.

AUGUST 30

Glossary

ace in World War I, an Allied airplane pilot who had shot down at least five enemy airplanes or balloons; German pilots had to have shot down ten enemy airplanes to earn this title

Boche the Allied name for Germans

conscription forced enrollment into the armed forces

dogfight combat between enemy airplanes

doughboy the name for an American soldier

isolationism the belief that a nation should stay out of world affairs

kaiser the German ruler

no-man's-land the space between two enemy trenches

observation missions airplane missions in which a photographer, or observer, takes photographs of the enemy's movements

over the top the moment when troops left the protection of their trenches to attack the enemy across no-man's-land

pacifist a person who believes peace should be maintained at any cost

shell shock the state of being worn out by the stress of battle

shrapnel an explosive shell filled with lead balls that explode in midair; the soldiers below were hit with the fiery lead

socialist a person who believes the government should control most property and production to ensure that all people have an equal share of goods

stalemate a point at which neither side in a conflict can take action

trench foot an ailment of the soldiers in the trenches, resulting from standing in wet and cold boots for too long

U-boat a short name for a German submarine

To Find Out More

BOOKS—Nonfiction

Barbeau, Arthur E., and Florette Henri. *The Unknown Soldiers: Black American Troops in World War I.* Philadelphia: Temple University Press, 1974.

Bosco, Peter I. *America at War: World War I.* New York: Facts on File, 1991.

Cooper, Michael L. *Hell Fighters: African American Soldiers in World War I.* New York: Lodestar Books, 1997.

Dolan, Edward F. *America in World War I.* Brookfield, CT: Millbrook Press, 1996.

Editors of Time-Life Books. *Our American Century: End of Innocence, 1910–1920.* Alexandria, VA: Time-Life Books, 1998.

Farwell, Byron. *Over There: The United States in the Great War, 1917–1918.* New York: W. W. Norton & Company, 1999.

Gay, Kathlyn, and Martin Gay. *World War I.* New York: Twenty-First Century Books, 1995.

Granfield, Linda. *In Flanders Fields: The Story of the Poem by John McCrae.* New York: Doubleday Books for Young Readers, 1996.

Grolier Library of World War I. Danbury, CT: Grolier Educational, 1997.

Hansen, Arlen J. *Gentlemen Volunteers: The Story of the American Ambulance Drivers in the Great War, August 1914–September 1918.* New York: Arcade Publishing, 1996.

Hull, Robert. *A Prose Anthology of the First World War.* Brookfield, CT: Millbrook Press, 1992.

Jantzen, Steven. *Hooray for Peace, Hurrah for War: The United States during World War I.* New York: Alfred A. Knopf, 1972.

Keegan, John. *The First World War.* New York: Vintage Books, 2000.

Kent, Zachary. *World War I: The War to End Wars.* Hillside, NJ: Enslow Publishers, 1994.

Kirchberger, Joe H. *The First World War: An Eyewitness History.* New York: Facts on File, 1992.

Kolata, Gina Bari. *Flu: The Story of the Great Influenza Pandemic of 1918 and the Search for the Virus That Caused It.* New York: Farrar, Straus & Giroux, 1999.

Leckie, Robert. *The Wars of America.* New York: HarperCollins Publishers, 1992.

Marrin, Albert. *The Yanks Are Coming: The United States in the First World War.* New York: Atheneum, 1986.

O'Shea, Stephen. *Back to the Front: An Accidental Historian Walks the Trenches of World War I.* New York: Walker and Company, 1997.

Rees, Rosemary. *The Western Front.* Crystal Lake, IL: Rigby Interactive Library, 1997.

Ross, Stewart. *Causes and Consequences of World War I.* Austin, TX: Raintree Steck-Vaughn, 1998.

Snyder, Louis L. *The Military History of the* Lusitania. New York: Franklin Watts, 1965.

Sommerville, Donald. *World War I.* Austin, TX: Raintree Steck-Vaughn, 1999.

Stallings, Laurence. *The Doughboys: The Story of the AEF, 1917–1918.* New York: Harper & Row, 1963.

Stewart, Gail. *World War I.* San Diego, CA: Lucent Books, 1991.

Tuchman, Barbara. *The Guns of August.* New York: Macmillan, 1962.

Uschan, Michael. *A Multicultural Portrait of World War I.* New York: Benchmark Books, 1996.

BOOKS—Fiction

Kudlinski, Kathleen V. *Hero over Here.* New York: Viking, 1990.

Lindquist, Susan Hart. *Summer Soldiers.* New York: Delacorte Press, 1999.

Martin, Les. *Field of Death.* New York: Random House, 1992.

O'Neal, Zibby. *A Long Way to Go.* New York: Viking-Penguin, 1990.

Skurzynski, Gloria. *Goodbye, Billy Radish.* New York: Bradbury Books, 1992.

Wells, Rosemary. *The Language of Doves.* New York: Dial Books for Young Readers, 1996.

WEBSITES

The websites listed here were in existence in 2000–2001 when this book was being written. Their names or locations may have changed since then. By starting with a search engine (such as Google or Yahoo) and entering *World War I Primary*

Sources you will be led to the websites listed below. The starred sites are updated regularly.

When using the Internet to do research on a history topic, always use a search engine as your starting point. This will help you avoid wrong leads and will cut down on the time you spend on the Internet. Your initial search will result in a list of matches that you can open by clicking on the various icons or buttons shown on the home screen. You will find numerous websites that are very attractive to look at and appear to be professional in format. Proceed with caution, however, when using websites for research. Many, even the best ones, contain errors. Some websites even insert disclaimers or warnings about mistakes that may have made their way into the site. In the case of primary sources, the builders of the website often transcribe previously published material, good or bad, accurate or inaccurate. Therefore, you have to judge the content of *all* websites. This requires a critical eye. A good rule for using the Internet as a resource is to always compare what you find in websites to several other sources, such as librarian- or teacher-recommended reference works and major works of scholarship. By doing this, you will discover the myriad versions of history that exist.

* The World War I Document Archive available at
http://www.lib.byu. edu/

* World War I links to memoirs, personal reminiscences, biographies, images, special topics, commentaries, articles, and many other resources available at
http://www.ukans.edu/

Life at Camp Funston: The Reflections of Army Sergeant Charles L. Johnston available at **http://www2.okstate.edu/ww1hist**/

The League of World War I Aviation Historians available at
http://www.overthefront.com/

World War I: Trenches on the Web: An Internet History of the Great War available at **http://www.worldwar1.com/**

The 1918 Influenza Pandemic available at
http://www.stanford.edu/group/virus/uda/

The American Experience: Influenza 1918 available at
http://www.pbs.org/wgbh/amex/influenza

Index

Page numbers for illustrations are in boldface

ABOUT THE AUTHOR

Adriane Ruggiero writes frequently about history, both ancient and modern, and international affairs. Her most recent publications include *The Baltic Countries: Estonia, Latvia, and Lithuania,* published by Silver Burdett Press; *The Byzantine Empire: A Cultural Legacy,* published by Golden Owl Press; and *The Crusades,* also published by Golden Owl Press. Ms. Ruggiero is also a frequent contributor to reference works such as *The Dictionary of the Middle Ages, The Encyclopedia of Ancient Greece and Rome,* and *Magill's Encyclopedia of Military History.* She resides in Teaneck, New Jersey.